MONETARISM AND THE DEMISE OF
KEYNESIAN ECONOMICS

Monetarism and the Demise of Keynesian Economics

G. R. Steele
Lecturer in Economics
University of Lancaster

St. Martin's Press   New York

© G.R. Steele, 1989

All rights reserved. For information, write:
Scholarly and Reference Division,
St. Martin's Press, Inc., 175 Fifth Avenue, New York, N.Y. 10010

First published in the United States of America in 1989

Printed in the People's Republic of China

ISBN 0–312–02473–8

Library of Congress Cataloging-in-Publication Data
Steele, G.R.
Monetarism and the demise of Keynesian economics/G. R. Steele.
p. cm.
Bibliography: p.
includes index.
ISBN 0–312–02473–8: $35.00 (est.)
1. Classical school of economics. 2. Keynesian economics.
3. Quantity theory of money. I. Title.
HB94.S74 1989
332.4'01—dc19   88–28184
                                                            CIP

To the memory of Margaret Nixon,
schoolteacher

Contents

Preface	xi
1 Introduction	**1**
2 Money	**7**
Money, motives and the market process	7
State commodity money	9
The origins of token money	10
The emergence of a central bank	11
The evolution of modern banking	12
Bank credit and money	13
A basis for monetary policy	15
3 The Quantity Theory of Money	**17**
The early beginnings	17
The Yale equation	19
The Cambridge equation	20
The demand to hold money	22
The 'naive' Quantity Theory	23
The 'sophisticated' Quantity Theory	24
The Quantity Theory and the UK economy	27
4 Money, Relative Prices and the Rate of Interest	**31**
Hayek and the Quantity Theory	31
Forced saving	32
Hayek's Ricardo effect	34
Dynamic considerations and supply constraints	38
5 Keynes's *General Theory*	**41**
The transactions and precautionary demand to hold money	42
The speculative demand to hold money	43
Liquidity preference	44
Money, income and the rate of interest	45
Money and prices	47

	Liquidity Preference versus Loanable Funds	48
	Liquidity Preference, money wages and unemployment	51
6	**Forced Saving versus the Multiplier**	**53**
	The multiplier	53
	Full employment and inflation	53
	Keynes's opposition to the concept of forced saving	55
	Keynes's defence of the multiplier	57
	Liquidity Preference, productivity and thrift	59
	General equilibrium: an uneasy reconciliation	60
	The stock of money and the flow of credit	62
	Liquidity Preference: a bond price interest rate theory	64
7	**Monetarism**	**65**
	The asset demand for money	65
	Equilibrium in the money market	67
	Money, ouput and employment	68
	The expectations-augmented Phillips curve	69
	The interdependence of monetary and fiscal policy	71
	Monetarism: the central propositions	74
8	**Control of the Money Supply**	**75**
	Public sector bank borrowing	75
	Private sector bank borrowing	77
	Banking School versus Currency School	78
	Money substitutes and the control of money	80
	Hayek and the rejection of monetary policy	81
9	**International Trade and Exchange Rate Policy**	**85**
	Mercantilism	86
	The gold bullion standard	87
	The gold-exchange standard	88
	Exchange rates in the post-1945 period	90
	The balance of payments accounts	92
	Monetary theory of the balance of payments	93
	Exchange rate targeting versus monetary control	94
	The myth of the balance of payments problem	97

10 Macroeconomic Demand Management — **101**

Keynes's view of mercantilism — 101
Lessons of the Keynesian experiment — 102
The formation of expectations — 103
Rational expectations — 104
The disappearing Phillips curve — 106
Crowding out — 107
The New Classical School — 108

11 Inflation — **111**

Money and inflation — 111
The stages of inflation — 112
Money and Keynes's *General Theory* — 113
Wages and prices at full employment — 115
Incomes policy — 118
Indexation and wage bargaining — 119

12 Free Markets, Monetarism and the Austrian School — **123**

The legacy of Keynes — 123
Macroeconomic theories — 125
Monetarism and the Austrian School — 127
Change, incentives and the market process — 128

13 Postscript: When Keynes was a Monetarist — **131**

Inflation and business activity — 131
Inflation and public finance — 133
The course of inflation — 134
Inflation and monetary policy — 134
International trade, exchange rates and currency markets — 135
Fixed exchange rates versus price stability — 136

Appendix — 139
Notes — 141
References — 144
Index — 149

Preface

This book attempts to integrate the most important contributions to the understanding of the modern money economy. The works of Fisher, Marshall, Pigou, Robertson, Hayek, Keynes, Phillips, Friedman, Muth and Lucas are examined against the common theme of money, monetary disturbances and real economic activity. The crux is the intellectual battle between the established tradition of the Quantity Theory of money and twentieth-century Keynesian economics. The central issue relates to the level of economic achievement which can be attained by the competitive process, and the impact of intervention designed to manipulate patterns of expenditure in an attempt to raise that level of achievement.

Monetarism holds centre stage for the reason that it has become commonplace to classify as Monetarist the belief that Keynes was wrong to deny the importance of the relationship between money and prices, as established by the Quantity Theory. Before publication of Keynes's *General Theory*, Monetarism by this definition was the view held 'by almost all economists except a few dissenters and cranks' (Hayek, 1978, p. 75). In more recent parlance, Monetarists are identified by the belief that inflation is caused by the 'demand pull' unleashed by monetary expansion; and by the denial of arguments which favour 'cost push' origins of inflation.

Keynes was a brilliant scholar whose influence upon academic economics and upon economic policy is second to none; but the importance of his contribution has been misunderstood, and the most dubious aspects of his analysis have had the closest attention. It will take some years to unlearn the bad habits of the Keynesian era; for students of economics not to expect that macroeconomic aggregates should lend themselves to purposeful examination. Until then, the teaching of macroeconomics will continue to offer the aggregate income–expenditure approach; albeit with increasing degrees of qualification.

So this book will be judged more suitable for undergraduates at Part II level, for the teaching of monetary theory and the history of economic thought. This stated, less advanced students should not be deterred by its unconventional approach. Whereas the simplified analysis of income and expenditure has readily lent itself to introductory courses, academic economists have kept for themselves the more interesting aspects of policy debates. If the reputation of the economics profession has faltered as the inadequacy of Keynesian advice has become demonstrably more obvious, the blame lies squarely with its members. Economists talk too much among themselves; and basic truths are hidden too often by excessively detailed, or even disingenuous, exposition.

Writing this book has been very much an exercise of indulgence and self-erudition in which most things turned out to be at least a little different from that which had been anticipated. To Professor V.N. Balasubramanyam, I shall always be indebted. Not only did he persuade me that I could write, and then that I had written, something of interest, he spent much time in showing how it might be improved. His generosity reflects that of his former teacher, Professor Milton Friedman, whose encouraging comments upon an early draft were opportune. I am grateful to my own former teacher, Professor J.C. Gilbert, whose care was especially valued because of the high esteem in which he holds the work of John Maynard Keynes. For their reading and comments upon final drafts, I am grateful to Glenys and Paul Ferguson. For the finished text only I am responsible.

G.R. STEELE

1 Introduction

> A man's mind must be indeed sluggish if, standing back from the work of his time and beholding the wide mountain ranges of past thought, he does not experience a widening of his own horizon. (Schumpeter, 1954, p.5)

Great economists are men of vision: not usually with respect to their originality, but for their success in achieving recognition and acceptance of ideas. Yet, there is a danger; with popularity, profound ideas can be reduced to trivial slogans. Too often grand philosophies are plundered to serve mean interests. In the twentieth century, this has been the fate of the rival philosophies upon which, in varying degree, the conduct of economic policy has been based – Keynesianism and Monetarism.

Each is grounded in the history of economic thought, but is the product of its time. Each has significance for economic organisation and for the role of the state, for freedom, for social justice and for liberty; all of which lie within the realm of the politician.

Keynesianism held centre stage following defeat of Nazi Germany, when its message was readily received by war-weary democracies. A young RNVR lieutenant, then unknown as a writer, expressed a common sentiment:

> I've not talked with anyone professing fear of the future: equally one does not hear of any active *determination* to make things better; there is a simple belief that they will be so, and that we have learned from war-economies enough to revitalise the peace. (Monsarrat, 1943, p.78)

These high hopes for post-war reconstruction, for greater liberty and a social cohesion supported by state health, welfare and educational services were sustained through almost two decades. Yet, as each year passed, aspirations became a little more jaded. Despite scientific, technological and medical advance, the simultaneous promotion of employment, economic growth, sound currencies and efficient international trading arrangements were elusive goals.

Such targets were not independent of the institutions of political economy. The order of society demands more than material affluence; but in the face of an ever present need for moral and philosophical bench-marks, politicians at every point of the ideological spectrum gave little time to these important issues. This was so with respect to the economic policies which were adopted, and in particular to the substance of their intellectual foundation.

In popular usage there is frequent reference to Keynesian and Monetarist economics, but more often there is little understanding either of the deep insights which these philosophies give or of their common pedigree. The profound analytical insights provided by both are either not understood or are ignored. Instead, they have been reduced to trivialities and to superficial slogans. Keynesian economics is now the synonym for state planning, public investment and income redistribution. Monetarism is portrayed as the ideological bastion of unbridled capitalism. These are but caricatures and this is particularly so of Monetarism, which is so often featured as the upstart, a dogmatic creed based upon ill-thought and underdeveloped ideas; a vulgar justification formulated to provide a semblance of intellectual respectability for reactionary politicians.

In reality, Monetarism has a substantial pedigree. It offers a framework of thought which has evolved over nearly three hundred years, but which is now extended to incorporate John Maynard Keynes's analysis of money into the traditional design. Essentially it is the revival of the Quantity Theory of money; its reinstatement as *the* basis for understanding the role of money and the effects of monetary policy. These developments are almost entirely due to Milton Friedman, whose work has achieved much more than the revival of an old tradition. Not only has Friedman made original contributions within that tradition, he has stimulated interest in other views on the role of money, which were left behind in the wake of the Keynesian revolution.

It requires no emphasis that a historical perspective brings greater clarity to modern policy issues. It enables fundamental ideas to be distinguished from pragmatic policy designs for specific circumstances. While the latter may outlive their usefulness, the former are essentially timeless though they will always be subject to greater refinement.

In many respects, the Monetarist challenge to Keynesian thought is being overtaken by developments stemming from the Austrian School of economics. Most notable among contemporary contributors is Friedrich von Hayek, whose work must also be set in a historical context involving the early Quantity Theorists, Keynes and

Friedman. The most recent and so the most controversial development is the formulation of the concept of 'rational expectations', which has provided a logical basis for launching an all-out assault on interventionist macroeconomic policies. The impact of this new idea is such as to warrant the title of the 'New Classical School'.

The purpose of this book is to trace the historical antecedents of Monetarism in order to provide an ordered perspective from which to judge its implications for contemporary economic policy. Chapter 2 considers the definition, origin and the use of money. No state intervention was necessary to promote the use of tokens, and the emergence of modern sophisticated banking practices was prompted by the subtle forces of the market process. State intervention played no necessary part but, where it was imposed, as sooner or later it generally was, it rested upon the basest of motives.

Chapter 3 reviews the antecedents of the Quantity Theory of money which provide the bulwark of Friedman's Monetarism. Twentieth-century developments established that, in the long term, money would have a neutral impact upon economic activity. Here the theoretical foundations were firm. Less certain were the immediate consequences of monetary expansion for relative prices and the allocation of resources.

Chapter 4 shows the relevance of the doctrine of forced saving to the arguments which link monetary disturbances to variations in output and employment. Hayek's contribution, together with his own particular criticism of the Quantity Theory is examined. According to Hayek, the Quantity Theory placed undue emphasis upon the effect of monetary disturbances on the *general* level of prices. Of much greater importance was its effect in distorting *relative* prices. Tragically, Hayek's views were to be lost to a generation dazzled by the Keynesian promise of a new dawn.

Chapter 5 investigates Keynes's critique of the Quantity Theory and his enunciation of the Liquidity Preference theory of interest rate determination. Many saw this as a major challenge to existing orthodoxy – which Keynes labelled the Classical School. Departing from traditional views of the role of money, Keynes's *General Theory* is important for introducing a new theme rather than for having produced a strident discord. Indeed, it has been argued (Johnson and Johnson, 1978, p.236) that the book was given disproportionate emphasis by the wanton interpretation of a theoretical work intended only as a stage in the continuing revision of earlier ideas. War, illness, and premature death were to deny Keynes the opportunity to influence the course of Keynesian economics.

The General Theory took on contemporary economics with its theoretical case for positive fiscal intervention; but not only was that case made upon the dubious methodological base of comparative statics, it was outlined within the context of very special circumstances – high chronic unemployment. Upon the assumption of freely available factors of production, all things are possible; but the economics of limitless spare capacity is no economics at all. Macroeconomic demand management will be recognised by future historians as an unfortunate diversion; and the lasting value of *The General Theory* will be judged to be with its chapters on money, which provide a link between the old Quantity Theory tradition and modern Monetarism.

Chapter 6 looks closely at a dispute which began in the early 1930s, when Keynes turned his back on arguments to which he had formerly adhered, in order to support the case for practical measures to ameliorate unemployment. Here he was deliberately controversial, riding roughshod over coherent and well-established analysis (see Johnson, 1975, p.116). He repudiated his earlier work with Dennis Robertson, emphasising the importance of fiscal expansion and the irrelevance of monetary measures within the context of chronic unemployment.

Intricate argument concealed logical inconsistencies. According to Keynes, fiscal expansion would increase the price of 'wage goods' (that is, consumer goods) as a result of diminishing returns. This would simultaneously reduce real wages and increase profitability. Yet, the concept of 'forced saving' was denied. Forced saving occurs when investment expenditure is financed by monetary expansion: as resources are reallocated to the production of capital goods, fewer commodities are available to consumers, and so forced saving takes place. Forced saving provided a key element in the Loanable Funds theory of interest rate determination. Later attempts to reconcile the Loanable Funds theory with Keynes's Liquidity Preference theory are critically examined, and the latter is judged to be an unwarranted generalisation based upon very special circumstances.

It required a substantially prolonged experiment of fiscal expansionism before Keynesian policies were to be seriously questioned. Chapter 7 shows how Monetarism took its cue from the failure of Keynesian analysis to come to grips with the coexistence of inflation and unemployment during the late 1960s. Anticipating these developments, Friedman was in a position to offer an alternative set of policy proposals. These were based upon Keynes's refinements to orthodox monetary theory; and upon Friedman's perceptive understanding of the relationships between monetary and fiscal policy, and of their likely impact upon the labour market in both the immediate short term and in long-run equilibrium.

The Monetarist objectives and strategy for monetary policy are discussed in Chapter 8, where attention is given to the mechanisms of monetary control, to the lessons to be gained from a historical controversy relating to the role of money substitutes, and to the wisdom of trusting government as the monetary authority.

Chapter 9 takes the main themes of the book beyond the nation state to examine the implications for international trade and exchange rate policy. The operation of the traditional specie-flow mechanism is contrasted with modern arrangements, especially those of the period following the Second World War, which were very much influenced by the Keynesian approach to economic management. Important issues relating to international balance of payments adjustment are discussed in association with the policy alternatives of exchange rate adjustment and monetary control.

Chapter 10 draws some conclusions from the lessons of the Keynesian experiment, from the Monetarist revival of the Quantity Theory of money and from the more recent rise of the New Classical School.

Inflation is discussed in Chapter 11; its origins, its typical stages of development and its ultimate cost in terms of sacrifice, expropriation and missed opportunity. The position taken in *The General Theory*, and Keynes's own further thoughts are shown to lie behind more recent cost-push theories. The use of indexation as an instrument to ease the restoration of monetary stability is examined, and contrasts are drawn between views expressed by Keynes, Friedman and Hayek.

Chapter 12 presents a critique of macroeconomic theory. Its pseudoscientific manipulation of aggregate expenditures is the damaging legacy of Keynes's *General Theory*. It misled the economics profession into making a claim to that which it could never possess; that is, the specialist knowledge 'to co-ordinate the efforts of all other specialists' (Hayek, 1960, p.4). Furthermore, the attempt by government to conduct rational macroeconomic demand management continues to threaten the microeconomic function of the market process in achieving efficient resource allocation.

Chapter 13 reveals that Keynes, too, once accepted the fundamental propositions of Classical economics and, in particular, those of the

Quantity Theory tradition. The widespread monetary mismanagement of the inter-war years not only created the immediate hardship of slump and depression, it established the conditions for 'a theory developed for the special circumstances of Britain in the 1920s to become accepted as a universally applicable theory of the failure of unmanaged capitalism' (Johnson, 1975, p.111). Without that conjunction of political strength and weak economic advice, which was a feature of the 1920s and 1930s, western economies might have been spared the pernicious diversions of Keynes's *General Theory*.

2 Money

> The origin of money is as elusive as the origin of language itself.
> (Moss, 1986, p.16)

MONEY, MOTIVES AND THE MARKET PROCESS

Once an armed robber has demanded money from you, it would be foolhardy to ask for a more precise definition of his terms. Yet, what might have been acceptable as money last year may well be rejected now. Some forms of money may be readily devalued by institutional practices; other forms will have a more lasting worth.

Any examination of the importance of money in its various forms must begin with a definition; and to arrive at that definition requires consideration of the nature of human action involving the use of money. Motives must be examined. The fact that money is commonly in the form of printed paper or metallic discs is largely irrelevant.

The use of money is as near universal as use of the air that we breathe. Only when air is threatened by pollution is a definition necessary to distinguish vital constituents from pollutants. Reference is made to clean air, where the emphasis is upon the adjective. So with money. Though the dictionary gives it as a noun, it is more instructive to concentrate upon the adjective: many items possess more or less 'moneyness', just as air may be more or less clean.

Anything which is used as a medium of exchange has 'moneyness', so may be called money. *Commodity* money may be distinguished from paper currency (token money) by the fact that it has a value separate from its usefulness as a medium of exchange. Commodity money is still in use; and it was used extensively until quite recent times.

It would be possible to rank different commodities by their market value: a goat might be ranked above a sheep, a sheep above a chicken, and so on. Any one of these items might serve as money. Its place in the above ranking would determine its purchasing power; and it would be possible to derive its price in terms of any of the other items.

In its purest form, money would be valued only for its purchasing power. Setting aside for the moment the source of its value, let one unit of money in this purest form be called a ducat. Suppose that a goat is worth ten ducats, a sheep eight ducats and a chicken half a ducat. The respective ratios of these (together with all other items of value) would establish a set of relative prices. The relative price of ducats (purchasing power) would determine how many ducats individuals might wish to carry (the demand to hold money) in order to facilitate normal daily transactions. Over time all prices, including the price of ducats, would be affected by changing tastes (demand) and production costs (supply).

The price of ducats is demand determined in the sense that, given the number of ducats in circulation, there is just one price at which demand and supply are in equilibrium (see Patinkin, 1965, p. 115); but how does a ducat acquire its value in the first place? This is an intriguing problem and one to which empirical solutions may be presented with a variety of historical detail. Their general pattern has been described by von Mises in his 'regression theorem' (see Rothbard, 1976, p. 167).

The value placed upon a ducat today is determined by its purchasing power yesterday. Its value yesterday was determined by its purchasing power the day before, and so on. This backward regression is ended by the juxtaposition of the 'last day' of a barter economy and the 'first day' of a money economy. The demand for ducats on the first day of money is thereby determined by its commodity value on the last day of barter. In its earliest use as a medium of exchange, a ducat had two components which determined its utility; a consumption use (as exists under barter), and a money use determined by its value under barter. The transition from commodity ducats to paper ducats (with no intrinsic value) which subsequently occurred will be examined in due course. Here there is one essential point; the use of money did not arise as the result of a rational evaluation of its potential benefits. It was the product of individualistic human action.

The earliest examples of trade involved the exchange of less saleable for more saleable goods; saleability increasing until each traded item reached the hands of its final consumer. The near universal recognition of the intrinsic worth of rare metals resulted in gold and silver becoming the most highly rated of saleable commodities. With the convenience of a high ratio of value to weight, durability, and low storage costs, precious metals became the basis for exchange. With such convenient forms, a money economy has the advantage of allowing an individual to trade without the need to find customers in possession of the goods which he wants.

Over the centuries, gold retained the confidence placed in it as a medium of exchange and as a store of value. The use of reliable methods of assay and of uniform dies to strike recognisable coins were later developments, all of which reduced the transaction costs of using money; mints belonging to the church and to respected individuals produced coins of known weight and quality, and competition kept the charge for work undertaken to a minimum.

STATE COMMODITY MONEY

Coins produced by the state have a long history; but their ascendency over privately minted coins came not from the greater efficiency of state (or royal) mints, but by decree. Events in England established a common pattern. To a monarch capable of usurping the church and setting himself as its head, nationalisation of the private mints presented no great problem. Henry VIII saw coinage as a device to raise revenue on a large scale and, by the second quarter of the sixteenth century, a state monopoly existed (Gould, 1970, p. 7).

The royal mints bought gold and silver using their own current issue of coins for payment. A deduction for seigniorage was made to cover operating costs, and more. This monopoly profit was taken by the king. The convenience of coinage, the absence of alternative suppliers, and the status of legal tender, ensured a continued supply of precious metals; but the temptation to increase the margin of profit proved irresistible. This was achieved by adding (increasingly higher proportions of) base metal to the coins. Somewhat surprisingly, debased coins continued to be accepted at their overrated fiat value but, again, the relevance of transaction costs provides the key. The inconvenience of having to agree upon an alternative value seems to have been largely responsible.

However, there was a widespread loss of credibility even before Tudor debasement reduced the intrinsic value of coins to zero. Not only did it prove impossible to attract bullion to the royal mints, English coins became unacceptable in foreign trade, while foreign coins were in ever greater demand at home (Challis, 1978, p. 96).

Following upon a millennium of stable currency, the adulteration of the English coinage was achieved in less than a decade (1542–51). Although debasement had had the desired effect of raising state revenue, it produced discontent and, ultimately, a refusal to deal with the royal mints. There followed the recoinage of 1560, the contrasting conservatism of the suceeding Elizabethan age, and the abolition of seigniorage in 1666.

Whether in England or elsewhere, the aberrations of periods of coinage debasement are to be set against the slow emergence of ever more sophisticated and efficient monetary practices as 'a spontaneous not a man made order' (Congdon, 1981, p. 2); a spontaneity which is revealed in greater detail in the origins and subsequent development of token money and, in particular, paper currency.

THE ORIGINS OF TOKEN MONEY

The basis for a sound metallic currency was established in England by the seventeenth century. Of equal importance to the abolition of seigniorage was an Act of Parliament of 1663 which made it lawful to export gold and silver bullion. Both measures precluded the fraudulent use of the royal mints. Indeed, they were the necessary safeguard which allowed goldsmiths to meet the persistent heavy demands of Charles II for loans. From this period, until the outbreak of the Second World War, the English currency set a standard for others to meet. Early confidence in the metallic coin gave the condition for the emergence of paper money.

From the 1630s, the practice grew whereby, for greater security, goldsmiths began to act as custodians of their clients' bullion. They provided, and charged for, secure warehousing. As goldsmiths were also engaged in the business of foreign exchange – trading coins of different nation states – the two activities made goldsmiths the most obvious source of finance for international trade.

In return for goods sold abroad, foreign merchants provided exporters with bills of exchange. These were a promise to pay at some future date (which gave time for the goods to be sold and revenue to be raised). Requiring more immediate payment, exporters would sell bills of exchange at a discount; and these were bought by goldsmiths with the ample funds at their disposal.

To protect themselves against the possible accusation of misuse of their clients' bullion, goldsmiths changed the legal status of the receipts which they issued. In place of warehouse dockets, promissory notes were introduced. These acknowledged an obligation to pay a given amount of gold on surrender of the note, but the notes were not a title to the exact same bullion lodged for safe-keeping. This freed its use in the financing of trade.

With their prudent balancing of the ratio of gold holdings to liabilities, goldsmiths won the public's trust – to such an extent that the notes themselves began to circulate in settlement of debts between third parties. At first, this had to be arranged by way of formal legal assignment but, eventually, the introduction of 'running cash notes' gave *any* bearer the right to repayment on demand. More liquid than promissory notes, they acquired the characteristics of modern token money, although with the extra guarantee of full convertibility into commodity money.

THE EMERGENCE OF A CENTRAL BANK

With the growth of their business and their increasingly larger holdings of bullion, goldsmiths looked for still safer depositories. Their natural choice were the most prestigious of their own kind, and so a few of the larger goldsmiths became goldsmiths' bankers; and the notes issued by these larger institutions came to be more readily accepted than those of the smaller goldsmith clients.

The deposits made by country banks with certain large London banks (the 'clearing banks') allowed settlement of debts by book transaction, and this arrangement was supported by the general preference, of the public outside London, to deal with local banks. Because London banks had few provincial branches, their notes were not (geographically) readily convertible into gold.

In England, one institution acquired a particular importance. This was the Bank of England which was established as a private company in 1694, with the specific objective of raising funds to finance wars in Europe. Its importance derived from the unique guarantee (of convertibility of the note issue) provided by the government. As the Bank's reputation grew, other large London banks began to settle debts between themselves by book transfers of deposits held on account at the Bank of England.

The dominance of the Bank of England was furthered by an Act of Parliament in 1707, forbidding (other) banking partnerships of more than six persons. Close ties with the state were strengthened further during the Napoleonic Wars, when interruptions to the international transfer of bullion made it difficult for the Bank to maintain convertibility. In 1793, the government approved suspension of gold payments and from that date – even without the status of legal tender (conferred only in 1812) – Bank of England notes circulated as token money with no guarantee of convertibility. Nevertheless, public confidence in the Bank, as the government's bank, remained strong. No circumstance could be imagined in which the Bank might fail.

The First World War and the financial crisis of the 1930s brought a final abandonment of convertibility in many countries, including the UK. The promise by the Governor and Company of the Bank of England to 'pay the bearer on demand the sum of ...' still appears on notes issued, but is now without substance. Formerly the note was a receipt, an acknowledgement of indebtedness, and an invitation to redeem its value for the gold equivalent. It is now an anachronism and individuals must seek for themselves to obtain convertibility at whatever price is determined by the market in gold bullion.

In all modern nation states, state token money is a medium of exchange only to the extent that people have confidence in its general acceptability. This confidence is destroyed whenever currency is issued to such excess that it becomes worthless. Germany (1923) and Hungary (1946) are examples. Whenever this happens, the public is forced to resort to barter and/or to use various forms of commodity money; scarce, high value, low weight cigarettes have often been used as a first substitute for worthless paper.

THE EVOLUTION OF MODERN BANKING

It is expensive to produce convenient forms of commodity money. Scarce resources have been saved by the use of low cost paper or base metal token money. Even so, there was enormous scope for the evolution of still more efficient means of settling debt: commercial banks continue to extend and to improve upon their services.

Banks accept deposits of state token money (hereafter 'cash') from clients who then use cheques to transfer funds from their own account to those of their creditors. A cheque drawn upon a bank account is acceptable (as were the receipts issued by the early goldsmiths) providing that the recipient is confident that the bank will honour that cheque. Here there are two types of risk. Although there have been many instances of commercial bank failures, the more commonplace risk attaches to an individual's own solvency.

Where this risk is felt to be high, it meets with a refusal to accept bank cheques without the banker's own guarantee. The introduction of cheque cards provides this guarantee in a convenient form, and effectively transfers the risk from the creditor to the bank. Credit cards have a similar effect, but provide the extra convenience of settlement of a series of transactions with a single payment.

Banking innovations have reduced, and continue to reduce, the use of cash, so that the amount which clients demand to withdraw for use in daily circulation constitutes (at any given moment) a small proportion of the total amount deposited with the bank. Like their goldsmith predecessors, modern commercial banks have put their clients' deposits to active use.

BANK CREDIT AND MONEY

Bank deposits are used to advance loans to governments, to business enterprise, and to individuals. In principle, these are no different from the activities of the original goldsmith banks, but the wider monetary implications must be understood.

Although they have no official status as legal tender, chequeable bank deposits have acquired the characteristics of token money. The flexibility of commercial banks in facilitating credit indicates that the total amount of money in circulation is certain to be related to the supply of bank credit. Clearly, the manner in which private commercial banks conduct their business, and the form in which the public chooses to hold its 'money assets', have important implications for the money supply. A brief illustration will clarify the most important linkages.

First assume that, in conducting its everyday affairs, the public will decide to hold its money assets (M) partly in the form of state token money (cash-in-hand, CP) and partly in the form of bank deposits (BD). Then, by definition

$$M = CP + BD \qquad (1)$$

Of the total cash issued by the monetary authority (C), part will be held by the public (CP), and part deposited with commercial banks (CB):

$$C = CP + CB \qquad (2)$$

Were the public to keep to a given ratio (a) of cash-in-hand to deposits at the bank, then

$$a = CP/BD \tag{3}$$

Were the commercial banks to keep to a given ratio (b) of cash reserves to total deposits, then

$$b = CB/BD \tag{4}$$

Substitution within the above three equations gives
$$BD = C/(a + b) = k(C) \tag{5}$$

where $k = 1/(a+b)$, and is known as the *bank credit multiplier*. If state token money (C) is given at £900, if commercial banks work to a reserve ratio of 20 per cent ($b = 0.2$), and if $a = 0.25$, then

$$BD = £900/0.45 = £2000 \tag{6}$$

and

$$M = CP + BD = £500 + £2000 \tag{7}$$

With a cash base of £900, the bank credit multiplier ($k = 2.222$) produces a money supply of £2500.

An alternative representation is obtained by substituting into equation (1) for CP ($= aBD$) from equation (3),

$$M = BD(1 + a) \tag{8}$$

and substituting for BD from equation (5),

$$M = C(1 + a)/(a + b) = mC \tag{9}$$

where $m = (1 + a)/(a + b)$, and is known as the *money multiplier*. For the values of a and b given above, and with the same cash base of £900, the money multiplier ($m = 2.777$) again produces a money supply of £2500.

If the magnitudes of a and b were fixed constants, the monetary authority would be in a position to exert the closest control over the money supply. By issuing more or less state token money (C) – sometimes referred to as 'high-powered money', although other highly liquid public sector assets, as well as notes and coins, are often included as part of the definition of C – the central bank could produce an exactly proportional adjustment to total money in circulation by way of the money multiplier. In practice, the values of a and b vary and their values are determined by many different factors.

The public's choice, between cash and bank deposits, will be affected by changes in relative costs and advantages and these will change with changing market conditions and as banking practices evolve. Similarly, commercial banks' cash to deposit ratios will be influenced by the state of financial markets, and by changes in the legal framework relating to banking. These and many other practical qualifications will add to the complexity of the bank credit multiplier, but the importance of banking practice (represented by the value of b) and of the public's choice of assets (represented by the value of a) is clear. Bank credit money is an important constituent component of the total volume of money in circulation.

Many interrelated influences will cause adjustments by both banks and public alike, with consequential implications for M, the *nominal* money supply. However, knowledge of the volume of money in circulation would be insufficient to determine how valuable a unit of currency is, in terms of its purchasing power. Money is no different from any other traded item in that both supply and demand are relevant in determining its value. Without knowing the strength of the *demand* to hold money, purchasing power cannot be determined. Moreover, changes in the supply of money have feedback effects upon the demand side; and vice versa.

A BASIS FOR MONETARY POLICY

All such considerations make the exercise of monetary policy an intricate operation. Indeed, a long-running controversy (which featured prominently in debates prior to the Bank Charter Act of 1844 and the *Report of the Committee on the Working of the Monetary System* in 1959) centres upon these particular issues.[1] Although debate continues, the weight of statistical evidence (which may be interpreted as giving support to the Quantity Theory of money) suggests that feedback effects are relatively minor (although their immediate short-term impact may sometimes suggest the opposite).[2] This being so, the nominal supply of money may be regarded as determined by a set of variables which are *independent* of those which determine the demand to hold money.

Were this not the case, it is difficult to imagine any basis for theoretical analysis to guide monetary policy. Those who argue that the money supply is 'demand determined' deny the potency of monetary measures, the basis of the Quantity Theory of money and the relevance of modern Monetarism. For the most part, such invective is political, being neither philosophically nor scientifically based. The contrary evidence is no less strong than that against the central tenet of the Flat Earth Society.

A more important criticism is that behavioural patterns are insufficiently robust. Certainly, the diversity of private market transactions and of behavioural patterns will cause changes in the values of a and b in the multipliers above. Major reforms, such as the financial deregulation within the City of London, will have their own impact. Indeed, the interpretation of changes within money aggregates is never a simple matter. Yet, while monetary stability requires no active intervention from a central authority, it does require that authority not to engage in activity which is itself destabilising. Given the will, there are principles which allow for monetary stability. This is the rationale of Monetarism. The relevance of the demand to hold money, and of the institutional determinants of banking practice and of the 'moneyness' of different liquid assets, are all central features of this modern Quantity Theory.

3 The Quantity Theory of Money

One thing is certain: the quantity theory of money will continue to generate agreement, controversy, repudiation and scientific analysis and will continue to play a role in government policy during the next century as it has for the past three. (Friedman, 1986, p. 65)

THE EARLY BEGINNINGS

The emergence of the money economy has been examined in detail. The evolution of increasingly sophisticated banking practices was seen to be guided by the market process. Banking is important to the money economy, but its presence should not be allowed to obscure more fundamental issues. A broad theoretical view of the money economy is of first importance.

The influx of American gold and silver, and the violent price revolutions of the fifteenth, sixteenth, and seventeenth centuries generated widespread interest and discussion, from which emerged the Quantity Theory of money. The first 'theoretically satisfactory presentation' (Schumpeter, 1954, p. 311) came from Jean Bodin in 1568, while important early contributions with regard to the circulation of money can be traced to John Locke (1692) and David Hume (1752).[1]

Locke and Hume are remembered as political thinkers within the Individualist School, holding the view that society is too complex to permit central direction. Man must be left to specialise in those areas where his unique experience leaves him best informed. With free competition, society gains from his pursuit of narrow self-interest; and the task of economic philosophers is to devise legal, administrative, and political institutions to support the market process. Of particular concern was the part played by money; the degree to which 'the increasing quantity of gold and silver is favourable to industry' (Kahn, 1984, p. 37). How trade and industry might be affected by variations in the quantity of money were matters of widespread interest; but the much more substantive issue – the link between money and prices, which was to become the crux of the Quantity Theory – was first stated formally by John Stuart Mill in 1848:

> If we assume the quantity of goods on sale, and the number of times these goods are resold, to be fixed quantities [T] the value of money [$1/P$] will depend upon its quantity [M], together with the average number of times that each piece changes hands in the process [V].[2]

These early considerations of the role of money came to be expressed in the form of an identity, that is

$$MV = PT \qquad (1)$$

where

M = the absolute quantity of money in circulation to meet the needs of trade.
V = the transactions velocity of circulation of money over a given period of time.
P = the average price (over a given period of time) at which items are traded.
T = the total number (or volume) of transactions taking place over a given period of time.

It is in the nature of buying and selling that time is required to search the market. The velocity of circulation (V) represents the speed with which market traders (both buyers and sellers) spend their money. Offers must be compared, terms negotiated. Generally speaking, where a market provides readily available information on all aspects of traders and their wares, money will change hands very rapidly in finalising transactions; that is, the transactions velocity of circulation of money (V) will be high. Conversely, the more the uncertainty, the longer the time required to complete any given transaction, and the larger the amount of money traders will wish to hold at any given moment in order to be able to complete their business. Here V will be low.

In a hypothetical world of perfect information and instantaneous deals, money would change hands at such a rate that the value of V

would become infinity. Money would circulate so rapidly that it would become too hot to handle; (even burning holes in pockets!). In such a world, barter could not be improved upon and money would become redundant. More realistically, the Quantity Theory assumed that this limit would not be reached.

It is because barter is cumbersome that money receives its special role. Money is unique among traded commodities, in that it is acquired not to be consumed, but to be held for a time before being exchanged. Where there is a general consensus as to the relative value of a unit of money, as against a vast multitude of traded goods and services, traders will wish to hold money in order to be able to complete their business.

This concept of money – its role in facilitating transactions – gave the basis for an explanation of the general level of prices. Without money, there would exist only relative prices (for example, a one-year-old goat is worth three new-born lambs). The relative prices of different items would be determined by their relative scarcities, that is, by the strength of demand and the costs of supply. Likewise, the ratio of the value of a unit of money to a given item (for example, one gold ducat is worth ten new-born lambs) would be similarly determined.

If the relative scarcity of ducats to lambs were to rise, the price of lambs would fall, and vice versa. Across all traded items, any movement in the *general* level of prices would reflect the average change in the relative scarcity of ducats to all traded items. Thus, for example, during a season of drought, harvest failure and consequent famine, the relative scarcity of ducats would be expected to *decline* to produce a *rise* in the general level of prices of traded items.

From the seventeenth century onwards the idea of the quantity of money as an important determinant of the general level of prices became well established. In the twentieth century, the Quantity Theory developed along two separate lines to give the 'Yale equation' and the 'Cambridge equation'.

THE YALE EQUATION

In 1911, the American economist Irving Fisher gave substance and shape to the idea that the general price level (P) is proportionate to the quantity of money in circulation (M). His seminal contribution was to argue that the velocity of circulation (V) is stable over time.

Fisher discussed in detail those factors which he regarded as important determinants of V. He argued that its magnitude is related to spending patterns and to institutional arrangements for settling debts, both of which change only slowly through time.

Yet, this provided only half the picture. With the main interest centring upon the effect which money has upon prices, it was essential to understand not only the forces influencing V, but also those determining the total number of transactions (T).

According to Fisher, transactions depended upon the (full employment) level of aggregate output, and upon the degree to which production processes are integrated. The higher the full employment level of output, the higher would be the quantity of goods and services produced and the number of transactions taking place. Moreover, the *less* integrated are production processes, the greater the number of intermediate transactions (and therefore total transactions) for any given level of full employment output.

With two of the four variables in the identity 'fixed' (see equation (1)) Fisher argued that the price level (P) varies proportionately with the money supply (M). Indeed, a very important corollary followed from this conclusion. For if prices were freely flexible, variations in money could affect *only* prices, and so have no impact upon real economic magnitudes. Although Fisher, and other early twentieth-century American economists (see Dorn, 1987, p. 11), drew attention to transitional periods of rising prices when 'Trade ... will be stimulated by the easy terms for loans' (Fisher, 1911, p. 61) the general view was that 'the amount of trade is dependent, almost entirely, on other things than the quantity of currency so that an increase of currency cannot, even temporarily, very greatly increase trade' (Fisher, 1911, p. 62). This principle was sufficiently well regarded to become enshrined in the literature as the 'neutrality of money'; a rather different emphasis from that which David Hume had given to the stimulating effect upon business of slowly rising prices (see Gilbert, 1959, p. 16).

THE CAMBRIDGE EQUATION

On the other side of the Atlantic, two Cambridge economists, Alfred Marshall and A.C. Pigou, gave a different emphasis to the development of the Quantity Theory. Marshall was especially unhappy with the attention that Fisher had given to V, which he felt was 'not the most convenient thing to be made the basis of investigations' (Kahn, 1984, p. 43). As Fisher had shown, this variable derives its value from institutional arrangements relating to the organisation of business and trade; but Marshall argued for greater emphasis to be placed upon the outcome of economic decisions.[3] How did any given individual decide upon the *amount* of money to hold in real terms? For Marshall, this was a matter of economic choice; and it is upon such choice that the Cambridge equation is based.

Prior to considering the Cambridge equation in detail, it should be noted that, in parallel with Fisher's equation, the Cambridge version offers a similar tautological structure, that is

$$MVq = PqQ \tag{2}$$

where

M = the absolute quantity of money in circulation to meet the needs of trade.
Vq = the income velocity of circulation of money over a given period of time.
Pq = the average price (over a given period of time) at which final goods and services are traded.
Q = the total number of transactions involving final goods and services over a given period of time.

Most crucial is the substitution of Q (transactions involving final goods and services) for T (all transactions); for it is this which determines the change in the description of velocity (Vq) and the price level (Pq). The implications of this change may be more readily understood if equation (2) is rewritten as

$$M = (PqQ)/Vq \tag{3}$$

Equation (3) points to the tautological relationship between the quantity of money (M) and aggregate nominal money income (PqQ). This shows how the money supply, aggregate income and the velocity of circulation are always inextricably linked.

To be considered alongside this *structural* relationship is one which is offered as a description of economic *behaviour* – the Cambridge equation – such that

$$Md = k(PqQ) = k(Y) \tag{4}$$

where

Md = the *desired* level of money holdings; that is, the demand to hold nominal money balances.
Y = aggregate nominal money income.[4]
k = the ratio of desired nominal money holdings to aggregate nominal money income ($0<k<1$).

Equation (4) is a hypothesis which may, or may not, be true, for it relates to the manner in which individuals (in aggregate) come to a decision about the amount of money which they *desire* to hold.

THE DEMAND TO HOLD MONEY

Whereas the Yale equation looks on money as a facilitating instrument for everyday transactions, Marshall sought to direct attention to the motives for the use of money. Similarly, while not being opposed to Fisher's presentation, Pigou felt that the Cambridge alternative was 'a real advantage because it brings us at once into relation with volition – an ultimate cause of demand' (Kahn, 1984, p. 46). The amount of money which individuals desire to hold at any particular moment of time will depend upon their level of anticipated expenditure. This, in turn, will be closely related to income.

While custom and convention will be factors determining the precise relationship between desired nominal money balances and money income, a host of additional factors is also relevant. The level and distribution of real income; the ease with which individuals can switch between money and other assets; institutional innovations such as the introduction of plastic credit cards; and the incidence of public holidays will all have a bearing upon the demand for money.

There is no limit to the list of factors which have the potential to influence the magnitudes of Md and k; but the crucial argument remained that such determinants would change only very slowly through time.

THE 'NAIVE' QUANTITY THEORY

The assumptions of the Quantity Theory inevitably led to the conclusion that the (rate of change in the) price level is determined by the (rate of change in the) quantity of money. The detail of the argument is as follows. The quantity of nominal money (M) in existence is determined by the monetary authority. This is the amount of money which is in circulation and which the economic system must accommodate: if this amount is not exactly equal to the amount people desire to hold, as outlined by the Cambridge equation (4), there would exist disequilibrium in the money market. The demand and the supply of money would not be equal.

Suppose that the quantity of money in circulation (money supply) were in excess of the aggregate of all individual demands for nominal money balances (money demand). Any individual finding himself with too much money would get rid of it, by spending it on goods and services. In other words, an excess supply of money has its corollary in an excess demand for goods and services. (The situation is again one of the relative scarcities of ducats and lambs, which was discussed earlier.) Given the assumption of full employment in the economy, the natural consequence of the excess demand for goods and services would be a rise in prices.

As the increase in prices is matched by the increase in nominal earnings, real income remains unaffected; but, at a higher general level of prices, it would be necessary for individuals to hold a greater quantity of money in order that they should retain the same purchasing power as before. Indeed, this is the primary message of the Cambridge equation, for rewritten as

$$Md/Pq = k(PqQ)/Pq = kQ \qquad (5)$$

where

Md/Pq = a measure of *desired* purchasing power.
Q = real income.

it argues for a 'target' relationship between real income (Q) and the purchasing power which *desired* holdings of money would confer.

The process of adjustment when there is a disturbance to money market equilibrium may be considered in these terms. An initial equilibrium shows the equality between the demand for and supply of real balances,

$$Md/Pq = M/Pq \qquad (6)$$

where

M/Pq = the purchasing power of a given money stock.

If the authorities (for whatever reason) choose to increase the nominal money supply to M', equilibrium is disturbed:

$$Md/Pq < M'/Pq \qquad (7)$$

M' is the amount of money now in circulation, and it must be accommodated. Individuals have no alternative but to hold this new amount; but this exceeds the amount they desire to hold. So, in general, individuals will begin to spend excess cash balances. This increased demand for goods and services will cause prices to rise. In order to maintain the same stock of purchasing power, there will then be an increase in the demand for nominal money balances. When prices have risen to Pq', and when the demand for money has risen to Md', there will be a money market equilibrium once again

$$Md'/Pq' = M'/Pq' \qquad (8)$$

with equality between the demand for and the supply of *real* money balances.[5] This causal sequence is known as the 'direct transmission mechanism'.

THE 'SOPHISTICATED' QUANTITY THEORY

Although the Cambridge School infused new life into the Quantity Theory, it was, like Fisher's equation, concerned with relating changes in the nominal quantity of money to changes in the absolute price level. It had nothing to say either on the source of the increase in money, or on the effects of changes in money upon real economic activity. 'Real' economic activity in this context might refer to the acquisition of resources (with saving from current income/production) in order to create capital goods (investment).

Ordinarily, saving (defined as income minus consumption) is channelled into investment through financial institutions. Where there is an excess of saving, the rate of interest (the 'price' of saving) can be expected to fall. This would choke off the supply of saving, increase the demand for investible funds, and restore equilibrium. Alternatively, levels of consumption might be affected with implications for saving and investment.

Adjustments such as these ensure the equality of saving and investment; that is, the supply and demand of real resources to create capital goods. Resources are directed *either* to consumption *or* to capital goods; and the rate of interest is the mechanism which ensures that the demand and supply of resources for both these ends are in equilibrium. The rate of interest, which leaves the demand for and the supply of 'loanable funds' in equilibrium, is known as the natural rate of interest.

Monetary expansion intrudes upon this mechanism by reducing the cost of borrowing. For any given level of saving, consider an infusion of newly created money in the form of bank credit. Prospective investors can call upon bank credit, as well as upon real saving, in order to satisfy their demand for funds. The rate of interest falls. Real saving would also fall (with a corresponding rise in consumption). Thus the effect of an increase in bank credit is to facilitate increased demand for *both* consumption goods *and* capital goods; and this increased pressure of demand must lead to an increase in the price level.

This causal chain, whereby an increase in the money supply results in a reduction in the rate of interest and thence to an increase in the absolute price level, is known as the 'indirect transmission mechanism'. It was discussed in detail in 1906 by the Swedish economist Knut Wicksell, although its origins go back a hundred years earlier.[6] Wicksell's analysis may be deemed a forerunner of Friedman's much discussed *natural rate of unemployment* concept,[7] so is worthy of close attention.

Wicksell's analysis is best illustrated by an example. Consider an increase in the demand for funds to invest following the discovery of unexploited mineral deposits. Mining entrepreneurs bid against existing borrowers for currently available saving. The price (the rate of interest) of funds rises. This may, or may not, encourage a greater volume of saving. Extra saving occurs if the community postpones consumption in order to take advantage of the higher rate of interest (although some entrepreneurs might well be discouraged by the rise in the rate). If consumption is not postponed, current saving is channelled to the highest bidder. In both cases there is an increase in the equilibrium rate of interest – Wicksell's natural rate.[8]

In contrast, consider the consequences of an increase in the volume of bank lending to meet the new entrepreneurial demand for funds. The rate of interest would not be forced up: the increase in bank credit would hold down the observed rate of interest below that rate which otherwise would have prevailed (the natural rate). Without the attraction of a higher rate of interest, there would be no additional saving, and so no reduction in the demand for consumers' goods. With the increased demand for capital goods (meeting new and previous entrepreneurial demands) and the unchanged demand for consumers' goods, there would necessarily be an increase in the overall demand for goods and services.

Given the assumption of fully employed resources, the increase in the demand for goods and services would cause prices to rise. But would this, as in the illustration of the direct transmission mechanism, restore equilibrium to the money market? Would the rise in prices remove the original source of excess demand? One thing is clear: if bank lending continues to hold down the rate of interest below its natural rate, prices, nominal money income, and the demand to hold money in nominal terms would all continue to rise through successive periods of time. The rise in prices which begins with credit expansion would only be brought to a halt by the cessation of bank credit expansion.

Only when the market rate of interest is allowed to rise to Wicksell's natural rate (where the demand for investible funds is matched by the supply of saving *only*) would equilibrium be restored. The amount of money in circulation would be higher, prices higher, and the demand to hold nominal money higher: but the rate of interest would be back to the level it would have held had the monetary expansion never occurred (although distortions caused within real sectors would be expected to delay this outcome). The final outcome is most important, for it shows that the rate of interest is a value determined ultimately *not* by the amount of money in circulation, but by *real* forces governing the decisions of savers and borrowers.

THE QUANTITY THEORY AND THE UK ECONOMY

The Quantity Theory derived from the pre-1914 world of slow economic change; where national output was determined by the gradual accumulation of productive resources; where competition was expected to ensure the full and efficient employment of resources; and where an internationally accepted gold standard with free convertibility of currencies made for monetary stability.

Developments of the Quantity Theory had incorporated interaction between the money market and real sectors of the economy, had debated the conditions which would be sufficient to ensure that money was neutral, and had raised the possibility that short term monetary variations might impinge upon the stabilising tendency of the price mechanism to clear all markets so as to achieve a full employment level of output; but still 'the theory continued to be built on the assumption of full employment as the condition to which the economy would approximate' (Johnson, 1975, p. 113) although increasingly during the 1920s its appropriateness had become questionable.

Rising unemployment in the UK attracted government concern although this related in most part to the system of administrating relief to those unemployed and in need, the ground rules for which required frequent rewriting throughout the 1920s (Tomlinson, 1981, p. 71). Contemporary explanations for the phenomenon pointed to the loss of overseas markets, increased competition from more recently industrialised nations, and to new technology, all of which necessitated a substantial realignment of factors of production.

An additional and arguably more powerful explanation for unemployment (so much more pronounced in the UK than elsewhere) rests with government policy relating to the value of sterling. Wartime inflation had caused sterling to be removed from the gold standard and, with peace, the restoration of international relations and the desire to re-establish London at the centre of international finance became primary objectives. Although the possibility of devaluation prior to the restoration of convertibility was later to be considered, the Report of the Cunliffe Committee in 1918 had recommended a return at the pre-war rate of $4.86. This figure was accepted with enthusiasm by the Treasury and the Bank of England and it became the major objective of government policy during the early 1920s.

In the first years of peace, the high demand for raw materials had reduced the value of sterling from its artificially pegged rate of $4.76 (March 1919) to $3.40 (February 1920). In reaction, the Bank Rate was raised, eventually reaching the peak level of 7 per cent in the early months of 1920. In timing at least this move was unfortunate. Its coincidence with reduced government spending, a deflationary budget and a decision to limit the note issue caused a precipitate downswing in the economy. Unemployment rose from 2.6 per cent in June 1920 to 22.4 per cent in June 1921. These were the prelude to the phenomenon of widespread chronic unemployment.

In 1925, sterling was restored to the gold standard and was freely convertible at the pre-war rate of $4.86. Monetary contraction had succeeded in reducing domestic prices over the preceding years, while in the USA a booming economy had helped by causing prices to rise there. Nevertheless, the new rate for sterling made British goods more expensive in world markets, and it was necessary for British prices to fall still further. This they did continuously over the following seven years, as a consequence of further monetary contraction.

Now, according to the Quantity Theory, monetary contraction causes prices to fall in the following way: from an equilibrium position (equation 6) the reduction in the money supply leaves individuals' *actual real* money balances below their *desired* level; that is

$$Md/Pq > M'/Pq \qquad (9)$$

Subsequently, in the attempt to raise these balances to the desired level, expenditure is reduced; but the only possible consequence (when it is *assumed* that output remains at its full employment level) is that prices fall. This reduces the demand for *nominal* money balances and equilibrium is restored.

How long it takes for this adjustment to take place was not a question to which the Quantity Theory addressed itself. In the long term, price stability at a full employment level of output was the prediction; in the short term, the effect which the reduction in expenditure might have upon output and employment lay in uncharted waters. More might have been expected from economists, as a retrospective view indicates:

> British economics lacked the confident grasp of applied monetary theory and the intellectual courage to insist that the exchange rate was crucial to Britain's problems and that continued overvaluation would make a solution impossible. (Johnson, 1975, p. 115)

It may be that this observation makes too much of the potential influence of academic argument. An alternative view may be closer to the reality of contempory government policy decision-making:

> it may well be the case that in defending their policies Treasury officials invoked the authority of classical political economy. But such invocation perhaps tends to obscure the mechanisms operative in policy decisions ... the explanation of the absence of a government expenditure policy geared to unemployment can be viewed ... as a result of the unavoidable constraints on the Treasury as a debtor. (Tomlinson, 1981, p. 102)

Whichever the preferred explanation, the institutional arrangements of the period are clear: to finance public expenditure, the Treasury would have had to raise money from the market at a time when the exact reverse had been deemed necessary, both to reduce the volume of outstanding government debt, and to maintain international confidence in the value of sterling. Although the damaging effects of the sterling exchange rate policy had been exposed – most notably in 1925 by J.M. Keynes in the pamphlet 'The Economic Consequences of Mr. Churchill'[9] – it had been to little effect. Change, when it did come, was to be brought about by events elsewhere.

The monetary contraction in the UK was less drastic than that which occurred in the USA, as a result of bank failures in the wake of the collapse of share prices on the Wall Street stock exchange in 1929. The refusal of the Federal Reserve Board to prevent such failures, and then to offset their impact upon the US money supply, exacerbated the situation. A fall in real economic activity was inevitable, but events were to go much further. Additional to the inaction of the Federal Reserve Board, policy itself played a part in generating the Great Depression out of events on Wall Street. Here again there is a view which seeks to attribute blame to the economics profession: 'In the months and years following the stock market crash, the burden of reputable economic advice was invariably on the side of measures which would make it worse' (Galbraith, 1961, p. 200). Begging the questions of its character and source, one piece of advice was that the US government budget should be balanced; that expenditure should match receipts. Moreover, in the worst economic crisis of modern times, the concern to maintain a strong US currency was considered as paramount. The parallel with the conventional wisdom applied in the UK a decade earlier is obvious.

Whatever the nature of contemporary economic advice, it is possible to argue that traditional monetary theory provided a basis for an explanation of the effects of monetary instability upon real economic magnitudes. Of particular relevance, not only to that current state of monetary theory, but also to a philosophy which was to gain ascendency almost fifty years later, were the views of the Austrian economist Friedrich von Hayek.

4 Money, Relative Prices and the Rate of Interest

The issues Hayek raised during the 1930s have their counterpart in the modern debates about the structural limits placed on short run macroeconomic policy. (Moss and Vaughn, 1986, p. 565)

HAYEK AND THE QUANTITY THEORY

In the 1930s, Hayek was the first to point out that monetary policy cannot be used to control *simultaneously* both the money supply and the rate of interest. As is well known, this piece of wisdom was rediscovered in the post-war years (after some considerable confusion promulgated by the Radcliffe Committee (Report, 1959)). More to the point, Hayek's insight foreshadowed the famous Monetarist Rule that the increase in the money supply ought to be maintained in line with growth of GNP.[1]

Hayek's analysis of the trade cycle – couched in terms of changes in the money supply – lends credence to the contention that the Monetarist Rule might serve as an automatic stabilising device. For these reasons, Hayek's views in relation to the Quantity Theory are of immense importance. While he accepted its general content, he was sharply critical of the interpretation that money affects *individual* prices only via its influence upon the *general* level of prices.

> I do not propose to quarrel with the positive content of this theory: I am even ready to concede that so far as it goes it is true, and that, from a practical point of view, it would be one of the worst things which would befall us if the general public should ever again cease to believe the elementary propositions of the Quantity Theory. (Hayek, 1935, p. 5)

Hayek argued that Wicksell was the source of the widely held but erroneous belief that, with the rate of interest always at its natural rate, the general price level would be stable (for example, see Keynes, 1936, p. 242). He contended that this would only be the case if saving is zero. If the latter were positive, then (with the rate of interest at its natural rate) investment, too, would be positive: productive capacity and output would expand, and (without an increase in the amount of money in circulation), prices would fall. If the general price level were then to remain stable, the market rate of interest would have to be kept *below* the natural rate: 'The banks could *either* keep the demand for real capital within the limits set by the supply of saving, *or* keep the price level stable; but they cannot perform *both* functions at once.' (Hayek, 1935, p. 27). The neglect of this insight of the limitations of monetary policy to achieve control over both the rate of interest and the money supply was responsible for a confused debate which was to occur in the early post-war period. Restated, Hayek's conclusion is that monetary policy may be effective in the control of *either* the rate of interest *or* the money supply, but not both.[2]

FORCED SAVING

Hayek contested the alleged 'neutrality' of money. Variations in money could instigate change in real economic variables; and Hayek's work emphasises the all-pervasive, short-run effects of changes in the money supply. Wicksell's analysis had ignored those effects, but his introduction of the concept of 'neutral money' itself suggested 'recognition of the fact that money *need not* be neutral' (Schumpeter, 1954, p. 1088). The subsequent search for the conditions in which money *is* neutral had only one logical outcome: for as soon as a set of conditions is established for ensuring monetary stability, it follows that money itself 'exerts an influence and hence that it is *not* neutral' (Schumpeter, 1954, p. 1089n). Hayek emphasised that monetary disturbances affected real sectors of the economy through induced changes in *relative* prices and interest rates; and he focused upon the mechanism by which these occurred. Central to his analysis is the concept of 'forced saving' which occurs when real resources are transferred (as a direct result of monetary expansion) from the production of consumer goods to the production of capital goods.

The origins of the concept of forced saving are to be found in pre-classical writings. By the early nineteenth century Bentham and Thornton had alluded to it; and between 1800 and 1850, the doctrine was elaborated by many classical writers including Malthus, Ricardo, Stewart, Torrens and Lauderdale (see Presley, 1979, p. 108). Hayek attributes this wide interest to the dissemination of Jeremy

Bentham's teachings, and he cites an early unpublished text. Bentham himself acknowledged Henry Thornton's *An Enquiry into the Nature and Effects of the Paper Credit of Great Britain* of 1802, as containing many of his own ideas (see Hayek, 1939, pp. 183–97). Developments continued on the Continent into the twentieth century.

In England, D.H. Robertson, in collaboration with Keynes, refined the doctrine in the 1920s.[3] Robertson's exposition of forced saving centres upon the analysis of business cycles. The extension of bank credit is seen as the means whereby the public is forced to reduce consumption, so that resources are diverted to the production of capital goods (see Presley, 1979, p. 96).

Forced saving also formed the basis of Hayek's *Monetary Theory and the Trade Cycle*, published in 1933. With an upswing in business activity, new inventions or discoveries, the opening of new markets led naturally to an increased demand for bank credit. Prosperity reduces the risk of default, and so banks readily accommodate this demand by reducing the ratio of reserve assets and increasing deposits. While new demand for bank credit pushes up the *natural* rate of interest, the expansion of bank credit prevents the *market* rate of interest from rising to that same level. With the market rate of interest kept, in this fashion, below the natural rate, there is upward pressure on prices. To this stage, the argument was exactly as expressed by Wicksell in 1898 (see Hayek, 1933, p. 111).

Hayek's insight was that all prices did *not* rise simultaneously. If they did, there might be little effect upon the real economy. Hayek's contribution (though owing much to Mises) was to emphasise the distortions which occur in the whole set of *relative* prices. The initial effect of new bank credit is to increase entrepreneurs' command over scarce resources. Their expenditure forces up the price of capital goods, which encourages the switch of resources from the production of consumption goods (commodities) to the production of capital goods. With the increased competition for labour and other inputs, wages and other factor prices begin to rise. The consequence is an increased demand for commodities generally, so that eventually *all* prices rise.

In this process, only those individuals whose incomes rise first (before the price rise of commodities) benefit, while those whose incomes rise *later* are harmed (a conclusion which had been reached by the French economist Richard Cantillon in 1755[4]). A measure of the harm done to the latter is the amount of their forced saving; the transfer of real resources (while the market rate of interest is kept below the natural rate) which enables entrepreneurs to increase their capital expenditure.

Upon the basis of these transmission mechanisms – a far cry even from those categorised as the 'sophisticated' Quantity Theory – Hayek argued that it is the 'distortion of the natural price formation ... on the development of particular branches of production ... which is of the most decisive importance to Trade Cycle theory' (Hayek, 1933, p. 113).

HAYEK'S RICARDO EFFECT

The unusual circumstances of the 1930s drew the attention of economists to the causes and implications of high unemployment. Hayek was not party to this understandable but unfortunate distraction. His particular concern was to forge a formal link between the business cycle and the persistent tendency of the market process to move a dynamic economy towards an efficient allocation of resources. Much later, with the revealed inadequacies of Keynes's static approach to the analysis of business activity, this was to emerge once more as an issue of keen interest.

The aggregations of macroeconomic analysis obscure vital questions relating to the adjustment of production to changing patterns of consumption and saving. The idea, that public expenditure might sustain an economy perpetually in a state of high employment, ran counter to Hayek's monetary analysis of the business cycle, which predated publication of *The General Theory*. Unfortunately, Hayek's ideas were only brought to full maturity in the late 1930s and early 1940s, by which time they faced a hostile onslaught from an economics profession which had been captivated by the new Keynesianism.

Causing particular rage was Hayek's argument that business prosperity would be brought to an end by *too much* investment expenditure. An overinvestment theory of economic slump was menacing to the Keynesian view that too little private investment should be supplemented by a programme of public expenditure. The controversy came to a head with 'Hayek's Ricardo effect'.

The Ricardo effect relates to the capital content of methods of production. It occurs whenever the price of commodities (consumption goods) increases and causes an increase in profits. This increase is greater for less capitalistic than for more capitalistic methods of production (defined in terms of n, the number of years before the value of a capital investment is fully realised in the value of the commodities produced). While greater profitability encourages increased investment expenditure across the full range of methods of production ('capital widening'), the incentive is greatest for the least capitalistic methods of production ('capital shallowing'). Reaction to this creates the Ricardo effect, as investments are concentrated upon less capitalistic methods of production, with the implied impact upon the capital structure of industry.

The confusion generated by this analysis is to be understood by the methodological differences between Hayek and his Keynesian adversaries (see Moss and Vaughn, 1986). The Keynesian comparative static approach allowed no appreciation of Hayek's concern with the disequilibrium nature of the cumulative process of capital investment and its consequences for business activity. Much is clarified (at little, if any, cost) by employing the modern terminology of investment appraisal with a detailed numerical illustration.

For any given period (say of a year) entrepreneurs must decide upon the optimal amount of net investment; this is the amount which sets the marginal efficiency of investment (declining with the amount of net investment in each period) equal to the rate of interest. The greater the amount of net investment undertaken, the higher will be driven the cost of capital which must lower the marginal efficiency of investment. Thus, in this period, the investment decision 'does not decide the *quantity* of capital that it is worth holding at the current rate of interest ... but *the rate per unit of time* at which the capital is to be acquired, or in other words *the rate of investment*' (Lerner, 1944, p. 333). Over successive periods, the stock of capital will grow, exhausting, in descending order, the most profitable opportunities for new investment expenditure. Not only will new capital face decreasing physical returns, the larger volume of industrial output will be sold at a lower unit price. Inevitably, the marginal efficiency of capital will decline; but while it exceeds the rate of interest, net investment in each successive period will be positive: 'The difference between the marginal productivity [efficiency] of capital and the rate of interest is the *force* which makes the stock of equipment grow or decline' (Lerner, 1944, p. 335). From these circumstances, it is possible to deduce the marginal efficiency of capital as 'the marginal efficiency of investment when the rate of net investment is zero' (Lerner, 1944, p. 335) which concludes our definitions.

With the following, it is assumed that the production of a given commodity can be achieved using capital with any expected duration of n years. Initially, investment in each mode of production is assumed to have been taken to the point where the last £100 of investment gave an annual internal rate of return (or marginal efficiency of investment) of 7 per cent. In full equilibrium (that is, with no further *net* investment taking place), the marginal efficiency of capital would also be at 7 per cent. Using discounted cash flow criteria, and assuming a constant annual net revenue from the sale of commodities of amount £x, we have

$$£100 = £x \sum_{i=1}^{n} (1.07)^{-i} \tag{1}$$

$$£100 = £x[1-(1.07)^{-n}](0.07)^{-1} \tag{2}$$

such that values of £x may be found for any method of production. The following is a selection from the values given by equation (2).

n:	1	5	10	15	20	25	30
x:	£107.0	£24.4	£14.2	£11.0	£9.4	£8.6	£8.1

Since these values reflect a capital structure which is in full equilibrium, it is not possible to deduce the profile of that structure. The analysis relates only to the last unit (here £100) of investment expenditure.

Suppose now that monetary expansion has the effect of causing commodity prices to rise by 5 per cent (that is, each of the values of £x given above is multiplied by 1.05). Clearly this must raise the annual internal rate of return (the marginal efficiency of investment) in all methods of production. Precise values may be obtained from equation (2), which now will have r (formerly 0.07) as the unknown variable. By a process of iteration, the following values were obtained.

n:	1	5	10	15	20	25	30
r:	0.124	0.089	0.081	0.078	0.076	0.076	0.075

In every case, the annual marginal efficiency of investment is above the original 0.07 which provides the incentive to invest in all methods of production ('capital widening'); but the incentive is greatest for the least capitalistic mode of production. Thus, while the stock of capital will be increased in every case, the bias will be towards the shallow end of the capitalistic structure. Increased investment will eventually reduce the annual marginal efficiency of investment in all methods of production.

It is here that the role of the marginal efficiency of capital is relevant. In this disequilibrium situation, there are no reasons why its value should be the same for all the different methods of production. For the Ricardo effect to be avoided, the decline in the marginal efficiency of capital, with respect to net investment over successive periods, would have to be greatest at the shallow end of the structure of capital, and least at the deep end. The presumption must be that any such relationship would constitute a special case; that with no systematic relationship the Ricardo effect would result in the concertina effect acting upon the structure of capital (that is, capital shallowing).

Hayek argued for the eventual dominance of capital shallowing over capital widening ('Hayek's Ricardo effect'?). A prolonged period of monetary expansion would stimulate investment expenditure in the manner described above. Not only would this depressced investment expenditure on capital goods would direct resources from the production of consumers' goods, and so cause the prices of the latter to rise still higher:

> so long as investment continues to increase, the discrepancy between prices and costs of consumers' goods must become progressively larger till the rise in the rate of profit becomes strong enough to make the tendency to change to less durable and expensive types of machinery dominant over the tendency to provide capacity for a larger output. (Hayek, 1933, p. 33)

As investments are switched into short duration projects, the reduced gestation period leads to an increase in the amount of capital stock (capital widening is the dominant force). This continues for a time, but shorter life stock requires a greater provision for replacement. So, while investment expenditure continues to rise, total capital stock eventually goes into simultaneous decline (capital shallowing takes over as the dominant force).

With the labour force tied to particular types of employment, unemployment is the result of this switch of investments. Falling income in capital goods sectors leads to a reduced demand for commodities and (given sticky prices) to further unemployment in those sectors. Reduced demand for capital goods to produce commodities contributes further to the slump. Eventually the recession bottoms out as falling profits from the production of commodities switch the bias to favour *more* roundabout methods. This acts as a stimulus to the production of capital goods, and to a rise in income.

Arguments in this vein caused great confusion among Keynesian economists (see, for example, Wilson, 1940 and Kaldor, 1942), within whose static equilibrium framework a higher level of investment could never be associated with a lower stock of capital.

DYNAMIC CONSIDERATIONS AND SUPPLY CONSTRAINTS

Hayek emphasised the supply constraints arising during the dynamic path of adjustment *before* a final equilibrium is reached. How is a fully employed labour force to be distributed between the different methods of production? Rising commodity prices create cumulative pressure against more capitalistic methods of production. Where investment in less roundabout methods is insufficient to arrest this trend, resource constraints may result in a failure to renew more durable machinery. It is this consideration which produces Hayek's Ricardo effect, but which cannot arise within the static Keynesian methodology.

Although Hayek argued that cyclical fluctuations would be eliminated if bank credit remained stable, he was not of the opinion that this could be recommended as a policy objective. 'The stability of the economic system would be obtained at the price of curbing economic progress' (Hayek, 1933, p. 190).[5] For economic progress to take place, forced saving (and its redistribution of income) was inevitable; but the benefits were to be had at the cost of an unjust redistribution of income from consumers to investors. Hayek saw an unresolved problem in the trade-off between that injustice and the benefits to be had: 'bankers will have to weigh carefully the relative advantages and disadvantages of granting credits on an increasing scale' (Hayek, 1933, p. 191). Hayek was confident in the likely development of monetary theory to shed light upon these problems, and perhaps to influence policy:

> I am of the opinion that in the near future, monetary theory will not only reject the explanation in terms of a direct relation between

money and the price level, but will even throw overboard the concept of a general price level and substitute for it investigations into the causes of the changes of relative prices and their effects on production. (Hayek, 1935, p. 29)

Yet, this confidence was to be undermined by the impact of rival analysis and conclusions developed by Keynes.

Had Hayek been correct in his prophecy, there might have been no place for the modern Monetarism developed by Friedman. Ironically, even though the impression, created by the publication of *The General Theory* in 1936, eclipsed *both* Hayek and the Quantity Theory for a whole generation, Keynes's analysis of the functions of money were to strengthen the old Quantity Theory and constitute a step towards the analysis promulgated as Monetarism.

money and the price level, but will even throw overboard the concept of a general price level and substitute for it an inquiry into the causes of the changes of relative prices and their effects on production (Hayek, 1935, pp. 29).

Yet, this confidence was to be undermined by the impact of rival analysis and conclusions developed by Keynes.

Had Hayek been correct in his prophecy, there might have been no place for the modern Monetarism developed by Friedman. However, even though the impression created by the publication of *The General Theory* in 1935 eclipsed both Hayek and the Quantity Theory total, while generation Keynes's analysis of the function of money went to strengthen the old Quantity Theory, re a considering a step towards the analysis promulgated as Monetarism.

5 Keynes's *General Theory*

> It is undoubtedly true that Keynes regarded the problems he was dealing with as problems peculiar to the monetary economy. (Fender, 1981, p. 132)

The General Theory has had an unrivalled influence in twentieth-century economic thinking and policy. It is regarded as a classic work, but along with many other classics, it has shared a common fate. Those who cite it greatly outnumber those who read it. Almost certainly, it has gained its reputation for the wrong reasons. Its lasting contribution lies not with the advocacy of a more interventionist stategy for public investment. That owed more to pragmatism than to any new understanding of the economy. Much more importantly, *The General Theory* contributed to the evolution of Monetarism.

The General Theory should be read for its sections on money, where the analysis of Keynes's motives for holding money were of crucial importance to Friedman's further refinement of the Quantity Theory. Thus the lasting contribution of *The General Theory* 'lies not in its refutation of the classical "orthodoxy" but in its application of capital theory to the demand for money' (Johnson, 1975, p. 116). Keynes contemptuously dismissed the long-run view taken by monetary theorists in the Classical tradition. In the long run, human uncertainty would always be resolved, so motives born of uncertainty were given too little attention. Money would function only as a medium of exchange. More liquid than any other store of wealth, money is ideally suited; but the price of liquidity is foregone interest. In a world of certainty, interest-bearing assets would be held without risk, so that no rational individual would hold money other than to serve transactions needs.

A central tenet of the Quantity Theory is that money is neutral. Although monetary disturbances would affect output and employment in the short run – consequences afforded close attention by Hayek – these revert to their former levels in the long run, once the original disturbance has died away. Ultimately, all money values change proportionately with money, leaving relative prices, output, and employment unaffected.

Keynes was critical of this preoccupation with the long-run equilibrium state of the economy, arguing that more attention should be given to immediate problems. The future was near and uncertain. How would individuals act when faced by that uncertainty? Here there would be complex motives for wanting to hold money; for with uncertainty, it is only in money terms that it is possible 'to discuss the effect of changing expectations on current activities' (Keynes, 1936, p. 294). While recognising complex interrelationships, Keynes introduced the tripartite division of the motives to hold money which became an incantation in the minds of succeeding generations of students: the transactions and precautionary demand to hold money; and the speculative demand to hold money.

THE TRANSACTIONS AND PRECAUTIONARY DEMAND TO HOLD MONEY

The transactions demand serves two ends: it is either 'to bridge the interval between the receipt of income and its disbursement'; or else 'to bridge the interval between the time of incurring business costs and that of the receipt of sales proceeds' (ibid., 1936, p. 195). The precautionary demand is to 'provide for contingencies requiring sudden expenditure and for unforeseen opportunities of advantageous purchases' (ibid., p. 196). The amount of money held to satisfy the transactions and the precautionary motives is determined by 'the general activity of the economic system and of the level of money income' (ibid.). In other words, it will be closely determined by the level of current income; so in aggregate across all individuals the result is essentially the same as the Cambridge version of the Quantity Theory; that is

$$M_1 = L_1(Y) \qquad M_1' > 0 \qquad (1)$$

where

M_1 = the transactions/precautionary demand to hold money.
Y = aggregate money income.

has the same form as equation (4) in Chapter 3.

THE SPECULATIVE DEMAND TO HOLD MONEY

In many respects, Keynes's arguments rested upon amateur psychology, rather than upon recognition of the behaviour of 'rational economic man'. This caused him to be assertive when, as Monetarism would show, analysis of the demand for money might have been more soundly based upon microeconomic principles.

Keynes's own inclination to venture his own fortune (and that of his college) in the stock market and in commodity speculation, led him instinctively to view uncertainty as the context within which decisions typically had to be made. Faced by uncertainty, an individual must make 'two distinct sets of decisions' in order to achieve his 'psychological time-preferences' (ibid., p. 96). The first set will relate to his income; that is, how much to spend on consumption and how much to save for the future. The second set concerns the form in which savings are carried forward into the future; that is, which assets are used to store the value of savings.

If money is used as the store of value, then savings remain readily available for immediate expenditure. The alternative is to carry forward savings in the form of financial assets redeemable at some future date. Inevitably, this must involve greater hazard in the context of uncertainty for, in acquiring such assets, an individual surrenders free and flexible control over savings (that is, he gives up 'liquidity' which is the characteristic of money). Compensation comes in the form of a rate of interest which is 'the reward for parting with liquidity for a specific period' (ibid., p. 167).

Given the existence of interest-bearing assets (and laying aside the possibility of default) why should anybody choose to hold money when the interest forgone is recognised as the opportunity cost of that preference for liquidity? It is the existence of uncertainty which gives the answer. Where an individual is uncertain as to the level of future interest rates, then there may be a rationale for choosing to hold money as a wealth asset.

Bond values vary inversely with the rate of interest. For example, if the latter were to rise from 6 to 8 per cent per annum, then a bond yielding an annual return of £12 in perpetuity would fall in value from £200 to £150. Clearly, if a rise in the rate of interest were anticipated, it would be unwise to buy bonds. Rather, it would make sense to hold larger idle money balances. Individuals behaving in this fashion have a speculative demand to hold money; they are speculating on the possibility of bond prices falling.

Were all individuals to share the same expectation of the likely future direction of the market rate of interest, then *either* the speculative demand for money would be zero, *or* else bond sales would be zero. More realistically, there would be a variety of opinion and, as the interest rate changed, so this range of opinion would also change. With a rising interest rate, more and more individuals would switch from holding cash to holding bonds, as the opportunity cost of money increased, and as the prospect of a capital loss diminished. So the speculative demand for money from all individuals would (as a rule) be 'given by a smooth curve which shows the rate of interest falling as the quantity of money is increased' (ibid., p. 171). Formally, the speculative demand varies inversely with the market rate of interest; that is

$$M_2 = L_2(i) \qquad M_2' < 0. \qquad (2)$$

where

M_2 = the speculative demand to hold money.
i = the market rate of interest.

According to Keynes, liquidity preference becomes absolute at some low positive rate of interest. At this low rate, any increase in the money supply (M) would be absorbed completely by speculative balances. In terms of the structural taulology used by Quantity Theorists (equation (2) in Chapter 3), the increase in M would be accommodated by a fall in the velocity of circulation (Vq), and leave the price level (Pq) unchanged. This behavioural reaction is to be expected because 'a long-term rate of interest of (say) 2 per cent leaves more to fear than to hope, and offers, at the same time, a running yield which is only sufficient to offset a very small measure of fear' (ibid., p. 202). This characteristic was to become widely referred to as the 'liquidity trap'.

LIQUIDITY PREFERENCE

Keynes's version of the demand to hold money – which he termed 'liquidity preference' (L) – is obtained by adding together the amounts of money which individuals desire to hold to satisfy the transactions, precautionary and speculative motives. The difference between Keynes's formulation (the sum[1] of equations (1) and (2)),

$$L = M_1 + M_2 = L_1(Y) + L_2(i) \tag{3}$$

and the Cambridge equation (equation (4) in Chapter 3)

$$Md = k(PqQ) = k(Y) \tag{4}$$

rests entirely with the speculative demand. While the Cambridge version presumed that the whole demand for money is proportional to income, Keynes's view was that 'this presumption should apply ... only to a *portion* of the public's cash holdings', and that the Quantity Theory was misleading in 'that it overlooks the part played by the rate of interest' (ibid., p. 194). Although reference is relegated to the penultimate chapter of *The General Theory*, Keynes implicitly acknowledges John Locke as providing these ideas for the Liquidity Preference theory. He quotes from Locke's *Some Considerations of the Consequences of Lowering of Interest and Raising the Value of Money* of 1692, which describes the value of money as derived from two sources; its value in use given by the rate of interest, and its value in exchange, depending upon the volume of money and the volume of transactions.

MONEY, INCOME AND THE RATE OF INTEREST

The monetary authorities decide upon the amount of money placed into circulation, and the public at large has no choice but to hold that amount. Thus the total amount of money *actually* held by all individuals taken together must necessarily be equal to the stock of money supplied; but this amount is not necessarily equal to the quantity which individuals *desire* to hold. There may be a divergence between the *actual* magnitude and the *desired* magnitude (that is, between supply and demand). Any such divergence will stimulate a reaction.

The consequences of this reaction are important. From a position of initial equilibrium, Keynes discussed the possible effects of an increase in the supply of money (M). The impact which this has upon the level of income (Y) and upon the rate of interest (i) ultimately determines the subsequent readjustment in liquidity preference (L): see equation (3).

Keynes illustrated two cases to show that it matters not whether the increase in M corresponds to newly mined gold (the first case) or to newly printed paper currency (the second case). With the first case, the value of gold produced (and therefore the value of new money placed in circulation) will necessarily be equal to the factor incomes and profits earned by all those engaged in gold extraction. Similarly, where paper currency is printed to finance public expenditure, the value of the latter will necessarily be equal to the income earned by all those engaged in selling goods and services to the public sector.

In both cases, the increase in the stock of money is *permanent*, while the increase in income is for the current period only. In a dynamic context, the corollary is that a constant rate of gold extraction (or currency printing) would generate a permanently higher *level* of income, but an *ever-increasing* stock of gold/money. Unfortunately, the full implications of this conclusion were not discussed within the static context of *The General Theory*, where Keynes confined himself to the comment: 'The new level of income, however, will not continue sufficiently high for the requirements of M_1 to absorb the whole of the increase in M' (ibid., 1936, p. 200). In other words, with a once only increase in the supply of money, income could not remain at its higher level, so that the transactions demand for money would fall, leaving more available to be used to purchase bonds ('or other assets'). This increased demand for bonds would have the effect of reducing their yield and causing the rate of interest to fall.

With the rate of interest lower, the speculative demand to hold money (M_2) would be higher: see equation (2). In addition, by its stimulus to investment expenditure and thereby to the level of income, the fall in the rate of interest would lead to an increase in the transactions demand for money M_1. Eventually, a new money market equilibrium would be reached with a lower market rate of interest, and higher liquidity preference.

At one remove, an increase in the stock of money by the two routes above has the same impact as a third alternative, that is, where new money arises from 'a relaxation of the conditions of credit by the banking system' (ibid., p. 200). Then, the increase in M occurs simultaneously with a fall in the rate of interest which, ultimately, leads to a new equilibrium, partly by induced changes in M_2, and partly (*via* an increase in income) by induced changes in M_1.

Keynes's view – that an increase in M and a fall in the market rate of interest would stimulate expenditure to raise the level of real income and liquidity preference – was radically different from established doctrine. The Quantity Theory gave no consideration to the level of real income. The economy was *assumed* to be at the full employment level of real income, in a state of long-run equilibrium, where there is no uncertainty about future levels of the rate of interest. As such, it would be irrational to hold a wealth asset which bears no interest. Under these circumstances, new money would not be absorbed by speculative balances. Rather, it would be spent and this new expenditure would force up prices. With prices raised generally the transactions demand for money would be increased and, in this fashion, the new money would be accommodated.

In disputing the relevance of these assumptions to a world where high unemployment was the common experience, Keynes presented a theory where the relaxation of credit conditions might reduce interest rates, raise real output, and reduce the level of unemployment. Yet, there were further complications, which were the basis for Keynes's belief that monetary expansion would be impotent as compared with direct fiscal intervention.

MONEY AND PRICES

The separate approaches – whereby marginal analysis is applied to price determination at the level of the individual firm or industry, while the Quantity Theory of money is used to explain the aggregate price level – constituted 'a false division':

> In a single industry its particular price level depends partly upon the rate of remuneration of the factors of production which enter into its marginal cost, and partly on the scale of output. There is no reason to modify this conclusion when we pass to industry as a whole. (Ibid., p. 294)

By this short statement, Keynes challenged the Quantity Theory's direct link between monetary expansion and the general level of prices. According to Keynes, the primary impact of monetary expansion would not be to raise prices, but would be to raise effective demand 'through its influence on the interest rate' (ibid., p. 298). This was the Liquidity Preference theory of interest rate determination.

Keynes presented his analysis in direct contradiction of the Quantity Theory, which gave no part to money in setting a level for the rate of interest. For Quantity theorists, the rate of interest was determined by real economic forces, as established by the Loanable Funds theory of interest rate determination.

LIQUIDITY PREFERENCE VERSUS LOANABLE FUNDS

The General Theory begat a controversy between two rival theories of interest rate determination which, though abated, continues yet.[2] The intricacies of the confused discussion reflect the complexities of the relationships between real sectors of the economy and financial markets. With both the established Loanable Funds theory, and the newer Liquidity Preference theory, the rate of interest is the crucial bridge.

The loan of a kilo of sugar to a neighbour carries with it the understanding that it will be returned in the future. If the loan bears interest, the expectation is that more than a kilo will be returned. If, one year later, 1.2 kilos are returned, the (annual) rate of interest is revealed to be 20 per cent.

This transaction can be set differently. The loan might have been of money (say, 50p) sufficient to purchase one kilo of sugar. If 72p is returned one year later, when the price of sugar stands at 60p per kilo, this is sufficient to buy 1.2 kilos; and the (annual) rate of interest is again revealed to be 20 per cent.

This simple illustration shows that, although the rate of interest is a *real* economic magnitude, it can be discussed in *money* terms. It is, of course, more common for loan arrangements to be made in money terms, in which case there may be some kind of legal contractual documentation. Where loans are raised either regularly or widely, this legal paperwork may take the form of a financial security (for example, a bond or a debenture) which may be openly traded.

Linkages between real and financial sectors are taken further with the recognition that among the more liquid financial securities are those which may serve as money (that is, as the means to settle debts between third parties). The most liquid of all – bank deposits and currency – constitute the purest forms of money; and against these, too, there will be a financial security. In the case of a bank deposit, the security is the legal obligation of the bank to repay its clients' deposits immediately upon demand; and in the case of currency, the security is the indebtedness of the state authorities (usually the central bank) towards holders of notes and coins. These purest forms of money may be distinguished from other financial securities by the fact that they bear no interest; or rather that the interest paid on the latter 'is a measure of their imperfection – of their imperfect "moneyness"' (Hicks, 1946, p. 162).

Keynes gave close examination to the real or 'own' rate of interest (of sugar in terms of sugar, wheat in terms of wheat, and so on). At any moment of time, there is no reason why own rates of interest (yield) should be the same for different commodities; but the highest amongst these becomes the standard to gauge the worth of any proposed investment.

The yield from a commodity (sugar, wheat) or asset (machines, houses) is drawn from a number of different attributes which apply in varying degree (see Keynes, 1936, pp. 225–34):

1. its production of new output; whether in terms of itself (for example, wheat) or in terms of services (for example, houses);
2. its wastage or carrying-cost; for example mildew in the case of wheat and storm damage to houses;
3. its ease of disposal; with an unexpected 'cash flow' crisis, the possiblity of quick 'liquidisation', with minimum capital loss, is a valuable attribute;
4. its change in value through time.

The decision relating to a potential investment in some particular commodity would be based upon the expected aggregate yield from these four attributes. Liquidity (point 3) and carrying-costs (point 2) are both a matter of degree and 'it is only in having the former high relatively to the latter that the peculiarity of money exists' (ibid., p. 239). From this, there

> is clearly, no absolute standard of 'liquidity' but merely a scale of liquidity – a varying premium of which account has to be taken in addition to the yield of use and the carrying-costs in estimating the comparative attractions of holding different forms of wealth. (Ibid., p. 240)

A comparison would be made between the relative returns from alternative assets/commodities. Whether money, sugar, or wheat is used as the standard of value is of no consequence to the ranking of alternatives; it is their comparative yields in real terms which is relevant. High yield assets/commodities attract investment; and, with continuing investment, yields fall as more sugar, wheat, houses and so on are brought to the market. Ultimately, in equilibrium, marginal yields are equalised.

The reason why particular significance is attached to the money rate of interest is because its decline (with respect to any increase in the supply of money in real terms) is at a slower rate than the corresponding relationship for the yield from sugar/wheat/houses. According to Keynes, there is an ongoing tendency for the money rate to remain the *highest* rate and thereby the one which acts as the general standard and 'which eventually knocks out the profitable production of the others' (ibid., p. 229). Why should this be so? Keynes gave three reasons:

1. Money is not readily produced, at least, 'so far as the power of private enterprise is concerned'. Its supply is more or less fixed, notwithstanding the inducement to increase that supply which a high yield represents. This first characteristic is common to all assets/commodities in fixed supply.

2. The utility of non-money assets/commodities remains fixed as their relative prices fluctuate; so substitution takes place, of assets whose relative price has fallen for assets whose relative price has increased. This is not so for money, which derives its utility solely from its exchange value. Where an increase in the demand for money raises its relative price, it also raises its purchasing power; and so, as a first approximation at least, the utility of money increases *pro rata* with its price. Substitution is less likely.

3. A fall in nominal prices must increase the real value of the money stock and so has the potential to lower its yield. However, this eventuality is discounted for several reasons:
(a) if the fall in nominal prices carries with it the expectation that prices will fall again, this must increase the own yield on money;
(b) money wages are sticky downwards;
(c) a general fall in prices may generate so much uncertainty as to 'cause a movement into cash' (ibid., p. 172), a feature aided by the negligible carrying cost of money.

It is the sum total of all the above considerations – crudely (but cleverly) summarised by the liquidity trap of modern macroeconomic *IS/LM* analysis – which is the *modus operandi* of Keynes's theory of interest rate determination. Yet the liquidity trap hides an ambiguity; for Keynes's repetition of the argument that the money 'rate of interest may be somewhat unresponsive to a change in the proportion which the quantity of money bears to other forms of wealth' sits within the same paragraph as 'The only relief – apart from changes in the marginal efficiency of capital – can come ...

from an increase in the quantity of money' (ibid., p. 234).

Throughout chapter 17 of *The General Theory*, a strong inference is that monetary expansion is undesirable because it reduces money's attribute of 'liquidity'. If monetary expansion were to rob money of this attribute, liquidity preference would show in the demand for some alternative commodity. (Historically, land ownership may have proved a suitable alternative: see Keynes, 1936, p. 241.) *Whichever* asset ranks foremost with respect to liquidity, the uncertainty associated with a business slump creates an extreme preference for this liquidity attribute. From this it is clear that nothing is to be gained from a monetary expansion which simply displaces money from that top rank.

High liquidity preference, together with constancy in the stock of money, leaves the own yield on money as the highest yield and other potential investments as also rans. It is in this broadest sense that liquidity preference *is* the key to Keynes's theory of employment; and the conclusion must be that Keynes's advocacy of fiscal intervention was not so much motivated by the futility of monetary expansion (as represented by stylised versions of the liquidity trap) as by his concern with the depressed state of business confidence. General despondency, which operates on both the demand side (via the low yield on capital projects) and the supply side (by raising the liquidity premium), is the heart of the problem (see Keynes, 1936, p. 316).

LIQUIDITY PREFERENCE, MONEY WAGES AND UNEMPLOYMENT

Though he was emphatic in putting forward Liquidity Preference as a rival to the established Loanable Funds analysis, Keynes admitted to having incorporated the rival theory in *A Treatise on Money*. The reason for his subsequent dissatisfaction with its central concept, the natural rate of interest, was his (mistaken) belief that it 'is merely the rate of interest which will preserve the *status quo*' (ibid., p. 243); a deduction from Wicksell's (false) proposition that the natural rate is that 'rate which would preserve the stability of some, not quite clearly specified, price level' (ibid., p. 242). The dynamic implications arising from new capital investment, increased output and the requirement for monetary expansion to maintain stable prices were incompatible with the static methodology of *The General Theory*. Hayek's denial of Wicksell's argument[3] was either unknown to or else ignored by Keynes, and the long-term implications of capital accumulation *per se*, and of the budgetary devices by which that might be stimulated, received very little attention.

Keynes believed there would be different natural rates of interest, each one corresponding to a different level of unemployment equilibrium; and so, the natural rate concept had nothing 'very useful' to contribute to his analysis. For an economy stabilised at other than the full employment level nothing in *The General Theory*, other than fiscal expansion, gives hope of movement. For this, liquidity preference and the stickiness of money wages were jointly responsible.

The high liquidity premium which attaches to money arises from its providing the standard in which debts and wages are fixed. It is the asset in which liabilities are incurred and in which future costs of living must be met. Any reduction in money wages would increase the burden of debt and so is likely to be resisted. For these reasons, wages are sticky in terms of money; from which comes the 'normal expectation that the value of output will be more stable in terms of money than in terms of any other commodity' (ibid., p. 237). But, in a severe recession, liquidity preference is high and the money rate will hold back the production of assets/commodities 'without being capable of stimulating the output of money' (ibid., p. 234). Only in the absence of money and 'any other commodity with the assumed characteristics of money' could 'the ordinary forces of the market' have the effect of reducing yields all round to some full employment equilibrium level: 'Unemployment develops ... because ... men cannot be employed when the object of desire (*i.e.* money) is something which cannot be produced and the demand for which cannot readily be choked off' (ibid., p. 235).

The high level to which liquidity preference rises in a recession, together with the stickiness of money wages, was represented as producing a permanent equilibrium state of unemployment; unless the government took direct fiscal action. Public expenditure offered the only chance of escape from economic recession, and *The General Theory* gave detailed attention to its impact upon the economy. In this, forced saving was brought face to face with a new rival – the multiplier.

6 Forced Saving versus the Multiplier

> Having been present at the birth of the multiplier, I should also like to be present at its funeral. (Clark, 1970, p. 54)

THE MULTIPLIER

Equal in stature to the Liquidity Preference theory of interest rate determination, which dominates the monetary side of Keynes's *General Theory*, is the concept of the multiplier and its role in shifting the economy between different levels of real output and employment.

The multiplier is defined by Keynes as the ratio between income and investment or in 'certain circumstances' between total employment and employment arising directly from investment expenditure. Driven by a 'fundamental psychological law', 'men are disposed to increase their consumption as their income rises, but not by as much as the increase in their income' (Keynes, 1936, p. 96). It follows from this that the new employment/income, which arises directly from new investment expenditure, itself stimulates new employment/income in industries producing for consumption; but new investment can occur only if 'the public are prepared to increase their savings' (ibid., p. 117) and this relies upon their income being raised. In summary, 'The multiplier tells us by how much their employment has to be increased to yield an increase in real income sufficient to induce them to do the necessary saving' (ibid., p. 117). However, the multiplier is a two-edged sword: it works towards augmenting both growth and decline in the economy.

FULL EMPLOYMENT AND INFLATION

With business confidence at its lowest ebb, with liquidity preference maintaining the money rate of interest as the highest of all yields, effective demand – the proceeds which entrepreneurs expect to receive from current production – is below the full employment level.

Investment is in decline and so it sets up a multiple decline in employment/income. This is the crux of Keynes's system, wherein lies the paradox of thrift, such that an attempt to increase saving (which, by the Loanable Funds theory would produce cheaper resources for would-be investors), would itself activate the multiplier to reduce income and saving.[1]

With these propositions, Keynes swept aside the market for loanable funds and the independence of saving and investment as determinants of the rate of interest, and replaced it with the notion of a *causal* sequence in which new investment would raise income, and income would raise saving. Against this background, Keynes emphasised the need for immediately practicable measures to reduce the high levels of unemployment of the 1930s. The realistic assumption was that there were 'men unemployed who would be willing to work at less than the existing real wage' (ibid., p. 289). His advocacy of public expenditure programmes rested on the belief that private commerce would show only the weakest response to monetary measures: 'the return of confidence ... is so insusceptible to control in an economy of individualistic capitalism' (ibid., p. 317). Fiscal expansion would raise output because, while it would tend to force up the prices of 'wage goods', there would be no such pressure upon money wages. The increase in prices would be a once only effect, explained by an inevitable reduction in labour productivity if labour were to find work within the confines of an existing level of capital stock. It did not constitute inflation which is an ongoing process. At the higher price level, real wages would be lower and this would allow unemployed labour to find permanent employment. Their unemployment is 'involuntary' in the sense that they would accept work 'at less than the existing real wage'.

If the supply of labour were perfectly elastic when there is unemployment, and if it were perfectly inelastic when there is full employment, then the Quantity Theory could be revamped as follows: 'So long as there is unemployment, *employment* will change in the same proportion as the quantity of money; and when there is full employment, *prices* will change in the same proportion as the quantity of money' (ibid., p. 296). Between these extremes Keynes conceded the relevance of a number of complicating factors such that, as output is raised towards the full employment level, the effect of monetary expansion would be partly to raise output and employment, and partly to raise prices. These complications included the belief that inherently less productive factors would be the last to be employed;

that some factors would become fully employed before others; that factor costs would rise at different rates; and that wages would tend to rise before full employment was reached.

Once full employment was reached, further additions to the level of demand would produce no further increases in output. Rather, there would be proportionate increases in prices as a condition of 'true inflation' was reached. Under such circumstances, Keynes anticipated a different set of policy problems but paid little heed to them in *The General Theory* where he suggested that his 'suggestions for a cure ... are of a different plane from the diagnosis. They are not meant to be definitive; they are subject to all sorts of conditions of the time' (Keynes, 1937. p. 222). Although high levels of public expenditure might become a permanent feature to sustain full employment (in an advanced economy), the crucial question of how that might be financed without creating inflation was neglected. This was not an immediate problem in the 1930s, although it has become the central issue of modern debate. Yet, was Keynes correct in asserting that the existence of unemployed resources gave a guarantee of expansion without inflation? Such an idea gave direct challenge to the mechanism of forced saving, with which previously he had been in full acquiescence.

KEYNES'S OPPOSITION TO THE CONCEPT OF FORCED SAVING

With some regularity, contemporary problems force attention upon the role of money, and the linkages between money, prices and real economic magnitudes. The impact of monetary measures upon the real economy is a recurring issue. While the pure Quantity Theory *assumed* the problem away, the doctrine of forced saving did not. With the latter, price rises were a universal feature of an expanding economy, while in *The General Theory*, the existence of unemployed resources gave a guarantee of expansion without inflation. The failure to deal with the impact of monetary variations upon real economic activity was a feature common to both the Quantity Theory and *The General Theory*.

In the 1920s, Keynes had made important contributions to Robertson's work on forced saving. Notably, he had persuaded Robertson that rising prices would lead to *induced* forced saving, although retention of the adjective 'forced' obscure a degree of volition! Induced forced saving might be expected from two directions. As rising prices cause individuals to reduce consumption expenditure, they may attempt to maintain the real value of their holdings of nominal money assets: so saving is increased. Furthermore, if rising prices reallocate income to those with a greater propensity to save, a second route to induced forced saving is created. In both cases, the ratio of idle money balances to real income is affected and it is this proposition which came to be regarded as the distinguishing mark of Robertson's contribution (see Presley, 1979, p. 32).

Notwithstanding this close involvement with Robertson and his own acceptance of the forced saving doctrine, Keynes came to express great hostility to the idea, and to his previously held views.

While, on academic grounds alone, it is difficult to understand the ferocity of Keynes's attack upon established theory, personality and purpose provide the clue:

> Keynes was – without any intention of slurring him – an opportunist and an operator ... theory was applied when it was useful in supporting a proposal which might win current political acceptance, and dropped along with the proposal when the immediate purpose had been served or had failed. (Johnson, 1975, p. 115)

So, Keynes was deliberately provocative in establishing new propositions in monetary analysis, seeking to create a schism between these and the orthodoxy of the Quantity Theory; and his repudiation of forced saving is crucial to an understanding of the true nature of the gulf which was to open up between Monetarism and Keynesianism. Keynes sought to establish that, together with the concept of forced saving, the Quantity Theory was irrelevant in conditions of high unemployment. An increase in the quantity of money or of bank credit would reduce the rate of interest, and increase investment, output, income and saving:

> Moreover, the savings which result from this decision are as genuine as any other savings. No one can be compelled to own the additional money ... Yet employment, incomes and prices cannot help moving in such a way that in the new situation someone does choose to hold the additional money. (Keynes, 1936, p. 83)

It was true that the extension of bank credit might affect the distribution of real income between different groups, but this could happen

Forced Saving versus the Multiplier

in any state of increasing output, whether financed by bank credit or otherwise. It could 'only be avoided by avoiding any course of action capable of improving employment' (ibid.).

Keynes attempted to show that, with high unemployment, *quantity* adjustments (that is, higher output) could be achieved without the price adjustments which cause forced saving. This is not to say that prices would not be affected. Indeed, higher prices would follow higher unit costs caused by diminishing returns to labour. However, involuntarily unemployed labour would acquiesce in real wage reductions, so that price increases associated with fiscal expansion would cause no forced saving; no diversion of resources into the hands of entrepreneurial investors. Although many were to be convinced, the case was made by default, for the analysis omitted to show the *process* by which adjustments were supposed to take place. Rather, alternative points of stationary equilibrium were compared with little discussion of the intervening stages by which the economy was supposed to move from one point to the next.

Investment *instantaneously* raised aggregate real income and the multiplier process provided the exact amount of new saving to finance that original investment. New investment expenditure would have no inflationary tendency because, at less than full employment, workers would accept *real* wage reductions, with the implication that the supply of consumer goods would be perfectly elastic. Use of a static framework of analysis meant that the implications of lags in the process of adjustment could not be considered.

This is in sharp contrast to the forced saving doctrine, where finance for new investment expenditure can only come from bank credit creation, with its inevitable effect of causing prices to rise. Additional demand generated by the increased production of capital goods cannot be met by the instantaneous supply of additional consumer goods, even given the existence of unemployed resources. Prices would be forced up because of immediate shortages.

KEYNES'S DEFENCE OF THE MULTIPLIER

The practical limitations of the instantaneous multiplier were admitted in *The General Theory*: Keynes even considered the extreme case where new investment expenditure comes as a total surprise so that there is, in the first instance, no output of consumer goods to meet the increase in demand. Then, 'the efforts of those newly employed in the capital-goods industries to consume a proportion of their increased incomes will raise the prices of consumption-goods ... causing a postponement of consumption' (ibid., p. 123). Clearly, it called for too much to use 'forced saving' rather than 'postponment of consumption'!

Nevertheless, these remarks represented no capitulation by Keynes, for he saw the postponement of consumption as temporary, lasting for whatever time is necessary to allow consumer goods industries to adjust to meet increased demand. Consumption then rises above its normal level – to compensate for the temporary postponement – before reverting back to that normal level. While recognising that these adjustments were relevant to the analysis of business cycles, Keynes maintained that they did not 'in any way affect the significance of the theory of the multiplier ... nor render it inapplicable as an indicator of the total benefit to employment to be expected from an expansion in the capital-goods industries' (ibid., p. 124), and, as if haunted by this problem, he states that 'Price-instability arising in this way does not lead to the kind of profit stimulus which is liable to bring into existence excess capacity' (Keynes, 1936, p. 288). Why not? For some unexplained reason, the unexpected abnormal profits would be universally recognised to be windfall gains accruing to those just fortunate enough to have products 'at a relatively advanced stage of production'.

For Robertson, this was unacceptable. The growth in demand would trigger further forces leading to further investment expenditure, so increasing the magnitude of price rises and forced saving. (This was later to be formalised as the accelerator principle.) Moreover, this enhanced deficiency of voluntary savings would exert pressure upon the rate of interest; a result giving direct challenge to Keynes's Liquidity Preference theory of interest rate determination (see Presley, 1979, p. 173).

In the 'classical' world of the Quantity Theory, money determined prices, while the rate of interest was determined by the non-monetary forces of productivity and thrift. Keynes denied the direct relevance of those forces, and produced an entirely monetary theory of interest rate determination, leaving the multiplier as the *force majeure* of the real economy.

Expectations of the future level of the rate of interest determined the balance between holdings of money and holdings of other assets; and the money rate of interest is established by the balance of the weight of individuals who feel that it should be higher, and of those who feel that it should be lower; but the analysis was deficient in that it did not say how it would be determined in the absence of any specific thoughts as to its future level!

Whereas Robertson argued for the accommodation of Keynes's Liquidity Preference theory within the traditional approach – by allowing it to provide the explanation for any divergence of the market rate from the natural rate of interest – Keynes was firm; and for Robertson 'Keynes's long-maintained determination to treat them as "radically opposed" has been to me from the beginning the most baffling feature of this whole controversy' (Robertson, 1966, p. 159). Even when criticism forced Keynes to face up to the question of capital formation, he continued to direct attention away from any immediate requirement for real resources; so that

> there was no wavering from the main principle that finance of economic activity is a matter of the demand and supply of money and that changes in the state of liquidity will bring about changes in the rate of interest. (Fletcher, 1987, p. 114)

For the remaining few years of his life, Keynes was consistent in understating both the influence of the rate of interest upon saving and consumption,[2] and of the influence of productivity and thrift upon the rate of interest. To have done otherwise would have diminished the importance of the multiplier, and have required the reformulation of the Liquidity Preference theory of interest rate determination.

The charge must therefore be laid that Keynes rebutted the logical position of the forced saving doctrine with one aim in mind. It was necessary to save his own theory.

LIQUIDITY PREFERENCE, PRODUCTIVITY AND THRIFT

Productivity and thrift were given new roles by the Liquidity Preference theory:

> Keynes did not so much *deny the influence* of productivity and thrift on the rate of interest but, rather, he *rejected the relevance* of the classical concepts of productivity and thrift to the determination of the interest rate. (Ibid., p. 129)

In Keynes's new presentation, the concept of the marginal efficiency of capital (falling as capital stock rises) takes on the role of productivity. The rate of interest sets a level for the marginal efficiency of capital, but it is one which gives no guarantee of full employment. The role of thrift is shared by two players, the propensity to save and the level of saving, each enjoying a distinct relationship with the rate of interest.

In this presentation, and unlike the Loanable Funds theory, changes in investment and saving have no direct influence over the rate of interest. Only in their impact upon the level of income and, thereby, upon liquidity preference, are they influential. For example, a fall in the propensity to save raises the level of income and causes liquidity preference to increase; the rate of interest rises to check expansion unless there is a policy decision to increase the money supply.

The difficulty in accepting this interpretation lies not with its logic but with its applicability, for it is centred entirely upon the paradox of thrift, whereby a decrease in the propensity to save (by increasing the value of the multiplier) causes income and saving to rise. It represents a world where there can be no adjustment to the ratio of investment goods to consumption goods without an *induced* change in the level of output and employment; a world where demand management supplants the market process in determining both the level and the composition of expenditure. It insists, for example, that an economy, at a given stage of scientific and technological development, can produce only one mix of investment and consumption goods which is consistent with full employment; or, in a dynamic perspective, that an economy cannot experience a different rate of economic growth without affecting its equilibrium level of employment. This is an implausible and therefore uninteresting context in which to settle the issue of interest rate determination.

GENERAL EQUILIBRIUM: AN UNEASY RECONCILIATION

When the instantaneous multiplier is set beside the dynamics of forced saving, the methodological differences between the Liquidity Preference and the Loanable Funds theories become paramount. One approach to reconciliation (see Hicks, 1946, pp. 153–62) is to consider both within the context of general equilibrium analysis, a structure disparagingly described as the 'human counterpart of celestial mechanics' (Shackle, 1967, p. 5). Aesthetically attractive, the perfect regularities of the Walrasian system offer the useful feature of setting the two sides unambigiously equal, to give a forced balanced view; a 'fair' position from which to judge the alternative arguments.

Within this context, no *special* characteristics can apply to the money rate of interest. It is a price which is co-determined with all other prices. Where there are n different commodity markets (of which one commodity, money, acts as the standard of value) together with a market for loans, there are $n+1$ prices to be co-determined. It is assumed that prices adjust by the process of *tâtonnement* and all markets must clear; but one of the $n+1$ demand/supply equations is redundant. To illustrate: in a two commodity world of apples and oranges, demand/supply conditions in one market (it matters not which) determine both the price of apples in terms of oranges, and the price of oranges in terms of apples.

Reverting to the situation of $n+1$ markets, it is of no consequence which equation is singled out for redundancy; the solution is unaffected. Where the market for money is eliminated, relative prices are settled by interaction between $n-1$ (other) commodity markets together with the market for loans. By this route the rate of interest will appear to be set in real terms. Yet, money is eliminated only in the sense that its demand/supply equations were not explicitly considered. It nevertheless remains that the solution within the other n market equations necessarily implies an equilibrium price for money, and it is possible to discuss relative commodity prices in nominal money terms.

Certainly it might appear that relative prices are first settled in real terms, after which money makes a late entry. So, this route will be attractive to the monetary specialist *pace* the Quantity Theory; but, in the general equilibrium context, this is unwarranted. Whichever market is made redundant, its importance is no more nor less equal to that of the other n markets. In overlooking this feature, the monetary specialist runs the risk of believing that the relative values of commodities are separate from the question of the value of money. To him the interest rate might well be discovered 'as a factor controlling the quantity of money (in some sense), and may not relate it to the general interest problem' (Hicks, 1946, p. 159).

By contrast, the specialist in real relationships will have in his province the market for loan capital, which allows him to discuss the interest rate in real terms. It was this same market which Keynes, in

The General Theory, chose to eliminate. With the market for loanable funds selected for redundancy, n commodity markets (including the market for money) co-determine $n-1$ commodity prices and the money rate of interest. Each commodity price is set within its own demand/supply context; but the solution is deceptive, for it is inevitable that the money rate of interest will be matched against the demand/supply of money to give the Liquidity Preference theory of interest rate determination. The redundant equation has eliminated its Loanable Funds rival!

Thus, while general equilibrium analysis makes partners of the rival theories of interest rate determination, no trace remains of forced saving; and the multiplier has no special role. Each is a meaningless concept in a world of general equilibrium. Two babies are lost with the bath water!

THE STOCK OF MONEY AND THE FLOW OF CREDIT

The idea of a link between money and the rate of interest is by no means modern. Indeed (as was referenced in the last chapter), Keynes gave acknowledgment to John Locke. So, although the monetary theory of interest rate determination is the most important theoretical contribution of *The General Theory*, it is original only in the sense of Keynes's success in putting across the idea; in converting many fellow economists, who had previously regarded the notion unworthy of serious attention (see Schumpeter, 1954, p. 1178).[3]

The confusion into which economics was thrown by the Liquidity Preference theory was largely responsible for the subsequent failure of monetary authorities to distinguish between money and credit. Tight credit was taken to imply monetary deflation, when often the opposite occurred. This widespread tendency to confuse money and credit is one which Friedman has variously commented upon (see, for example, Friedman, 1969, p. 75; 1986, p. 28).

With personal financial arrangements there is rarely this confusion. Most individuals would recognise that, in obtaining credit, they become indebted to others. They hold a liability. They would also recognise that the exact opposite occurs when they acquire money. They hold an asset. Less obvious is the special attribute of a bank, which is that its liabilities serve as money.

By extending credit (in the way of loans) banks create new liabilities (current account deposits). With money defined as notes and coins in circulation, plus the amount of bank credit extended, Liquidity Preference theory works with the *stock* of money extant at any moment of time. The situation is rather different with respect to its rival theory, where non-bank credit may be regarded as synonymous with loanable funds. (Non-bank credit is defined as that which cannot be used by the credit-holder to settle a debt with a third party.) Non-bank credit may be extended either upon the basis of non-consumption of current income (real saving) or upon the basis of realisation of wealth assets (dis-saving); but if it were ever extended upon the basis of negotiable IOUs, the 'non-bank' would have to be redesignated 'bank'! It is here that the distinction between money and credit is drawn.

Credit is a flow concept and, from whichever source it is available, it is charged for per unit of time, at whichever rate of interest is set within the market for loanable funds. This is not so for money, which is measured as a stock. The price of money is determined at a moment of time by the number of commodities which must be given up in order to possess a unit of money. However, the linkages between money and credit (or, rather, bank credit) gives some support to the interpretation that the Liquidity Preference verses Loanable Funds dispute is a shadow-fight, with the former providing a snapshot of the changing panorama displayed by the latter.[4] While it does less damage to the original propositions than the general equilibrium approach, this view is charitable to Keynes.

The snapshot interpretation has been exposed by way of a fishing analogy (see Modigliani, 1944, p. 237). The snapshot shows the price of fish on a given day, determined by demand and that day's catch. A series of daily snapshots would show considerable variation. However, if the question is asked why fluctuations are around a particular mean price level, rather than another ten times as high, a more fundamental explanation is required than fishermen's luck.

The number of fishermen and the equipment which they use change very little through time. These are determined by the condition that average returns must be sufficiently high to make fishing an attractive occupation/investment. What is true of the price of fish is true of the price of credit; and the statement that the daily rate is determined by the demand/supply of money (that is, the Liquidity Preference theory) does not advance understanding of the true determinants of the interest rate. These comprise far more fundamental factors, both technological and psychological, which are subsumed in the propensity to save and the demand for loanable funds.

LIQUIDITY PREFERENCE: A BOND PRICE INTEREST RATE THEORY

Keynes set his Liquidity Preference theory in the context of constant commodity prices; where an expansion of the money supply is not inflationary. Rather, monetary expansion changes the price of money, not in terms of the amount of commodities which must be given up in order to possess a unit of money, but in terms of bonds. An expansion of the money supply reduces the price of money (in terms of bonds) and increases the price of bonds (in terms of money).

The bond price is the linkage between money and the rate of interest. Liquidity Preference is only a theory of interest rate determination to the extent that an interest rate is derived as the ratio of the nominal return (in perpetuity) on an undated bond to the price of the bond. Resolution of the debate ultimately turns on causality. Does this ratio determine the rate of interest (in which case the Liquidity Preference theory is saved), or does the rate of interest determine this ratio (in which case the Loanable Funds theory is saved)?

Keynes's discussion of the determinants of yield (or own rate of interest) on commodities provides the clue.[5] For the tendency of the money rate to remain the highest rate (in the context of a business slump, which has reduced yields across all commodities) would be wrongly interpreted as giving confirmation to the Liquidity Preference theory of interest rate determination. While the money rate remains the highest rate, it may appear that liquidity preference sets the level against which other yields are compared; but the situation is not a sustainable equilibrium.

Reallocation of investments (however slow) will eventually close this gap and bring all yields into line with the availability of loanable funds; and even while the money rate may be the highest rate, it leads as the bow wave of the rate set by the demand and supply of loanable funds. In this sense, the Liquidity Preference theory of interest rate determination misrepresents the situation; but the justification which it provided for an asset demand for money did serve to advance monetary analysis. It was this aspect of Keynes's *General Theory* which had a major part in the development of the theoretical structure of Monetarism.

7 Monetarism

Money itself rapidly loses the attribute of 'liquidity' if its future supply is expected to undergo sharp changes. (Keynes, 1936, p. 241 fn. 1)

THE ASSET DEMAND FOR MONEY

Although found wanting as a theory of interest rate detemination, Keynes's analysis of the demand for money represents an important stage in the development of Monetarism. In regarding money as one asset among many competing alternatives, Monetarism has drawn upon Keynes's insight as to the wider motives for holding money. In *The General Theory*, Keynes concentrated upon the choice between just two assets, money and bonds, and discussed the speculative demand for money in that context. This was a simplification, legitimate for exposition, but one which was taken too literally by later exponents of Keynesianism. Monetarism relaxed that simplifying assumption. At the same time, it placed Keynes's monetary analysis into its true context, that of an amplication of the original Quantity Theory.

Monetarism relies much more upon economics than upon assumptions relating to psychological propensities. By incorporating rational human action into the analysis (to a far greater extent than Keynes's own propositions), Monetarism has re-enforced the proposition that the income velocity of circulation is stable.

Accepting that individuals have many different motives for wanting to hold money, Monetarism directs attention to the question 'How much?' The question is considered in the context of an individual acting as a rational economic agent, seeking to maximise his welfare. He receives income, not all of which he consumes, so that he accumulates a stock of wealth in the form of various types of assets (his 'asset portfolio').

In adjusting the amounts of different assets within the portfolio, an individual must decide in which proportions they are to be held. Each brings utility in the form of pecuniary and non-pecuniary returns, and the valuation of the different characteristics of each asset determines the amount of each held. Within every portfolio, the mix of assets is structured to maximise utility, and with changing conditions is restructured to continue to meet that objective.

Any event which directly induces a change in the rate of return on any one asset will have implications for the whole portfolio. This is because total utility is maximised when each of the assets provides an equal amount of utility at the margin (per unit cost). A marginal adjustment of any one asset will require simultaneous adjustment of every other asset. The relative merits of alternative assets will lie in the characteristics of their yield; 'and it is essentially these differences that are fundamental to the "utility" of a particular structure of wealth' (Friedman, 1956, p. 7).

Monetarism attempts to identify the most important factors which determine the structure of wealth. Since the demand for any asset is determined by the relative utility of its own yield considered against the yield of other assets, the demand to hold money is derived from the chosen structure of wealth.

Moving beyond Keynes's two asset portfolio, Friedman identified the main alternatives to money as bonds, equities, durable goods, and human capital.[1] Thus the *ratio* of desired money balances to nominal income (Md/Y), is determined by the attributes of alternative portfolio assets. Important determinants of the demand for money are the rates of return to bonds (rb), equities (re), and durable goods (the latter represented by the proportionate rate of change in prices). Also included are the general level of prices (P) (which reflects the purchasing power of money), and the total of all wealth assets held (W). Thus

$$Md/Y = f(rb, re, \dot{P}/P, P, W) \tag{1}$$

or

$$Md = f(rb, re, \dot{P}/P, P, W).Y \tag{2}$$

where

$\dot{P}/P$ = the proportionate rate of change of prices.

This is the demand for money equation in its traditional Quantity Theory form. If equation (2) is compared with the Cambridge equation

$$Md = k.Y \tag{3}$$

the difference between the traditional Quantity Theory and modern Monetarism becomes explicit: with the latter, the desired ratio of money holdings to money income (that is k, the reciprocal of the income velocity of circulation) is governed by a number of specific determinants.

No longer is the thesis that a constant ratio gives a strictly proportional relationship between the demand for money and nominal money income. In its place, reflecting a more extensive interplay of economic forces, Monetarism states that this ratio will be subject to systematic variation, as utility-conscious individuals adjust and readjust the composition of their asset portfolios. Net wealth, rather than current income, is the primary basis upon which the demand for money is decided, although the latter may serve in statistical studies as a more readily available index of wealth:

> The emphasis on income as a surrogate for wealth, rather than as a measure of the 'work' to be done by money, is perhaps the basic conceptual difference between the more recent analyses of the demand for money and the earlier versions of the quantity theory. (Friedman, 1986, p. 21)

Whereas the traditional Quantity Theorists argued for the long-run constancy of the income velocity of circulation of money, their modern counterparts believe instead that those factors determining the income velocity are held in a relationship which is complex, but inherently stable.

EQUILIBRIUM IN THE MONEY MARKET

The demand to hold money is independently determined by a variety of factors, while the supply of money can be varied at the discretion of monetary authorities. Thus, the amount of money placed into circulation is the amount which the general public has no choice but to hold. If that amount is, say, greater than the aggregate demand to hold money, then there is disequilibrium in the money market. Every individual holding money in excess of requirements would then take action to reduce those holdings. For each individual taken separately, it is true that 'he can control the amount of cash that he holds. He can increase his cash balances by selling some assets for cash or spending less than he receives from other sources. He can reduce his cash balances by spending ... more than he receives' – but for all individuals taken together – 'they would simply be playing a game of musical chairs' (Friedman, 1959, p. 609).[2] Where the net effect of *all* individual adjustments is an *attempted* reduction in the aggregate amount of money held across all asset portfolios, the flow of expenditure would be raised and prices driven up. With the general level of prices appearing as one of the determinants of the demand to hold money, the latter also would begin to rise. Eventually a new equilibrium will be reached where the increase in prices is sufficient to take up the original discrepancy between the demand and supply of money.

Whereas Keynes viewed monetary expansion (in excess of the demand to hold money) as having its immediate impact upon financial markets, pushing up the price of bonds, Monetarism holds that the adjustment is far more extensive, affecting not only near money and other financial assets, but non-financial assets as well. Monetary expansion would stimulate a *general* rise in prices as people *attempt* to switch out of money and into other assets (land, houses, consumer durables, and so on).

With this general rise in prices (a factor discounted by Keynes's analysis) there would be a *pro rata* increase in the transactions demand for money and, therefore, no surplus to fuel speculative balances and to force down the rate of interest. In short, the attempt to reduce holdings of money sets in train a process which leads ultimately to that attempt being abandoned. Thus, according to Friedman, the rate of interest would be unaffected by an increase in the money supply and so, somewhat ironically, the price of bonds would be the one price to remain *unaffected* by that increase.

MONEY, OUTPUT AND EMPLOYMENT

The interrelationship, between money, prices, output and employment at and around the full employment level, was not an issue which received much attention in *The General Theory*. It evoked no contemporary interest during the 1930s, nor after, until the publication in 1958 of a paper by A.W. Phillips. This was an empirical study of wage and employment data for the UK for the period 1861–1957. It gave the stimulus to economists seeking to explain the tendency to inflation in periods of prolonged economic prosperity.

Phillips found a negative non-linear relationship between the rate of change in money wage rates and the percentage rate of unemployment. A notable secondary feature of the data was their tendency to track business cycle anti-clockwise loops around the fitted curve. The non-linear relationship was explained as follows;

> When the demand for labour is high and there are few unemployed we should expect employers to bid up rates quite rapidly ... On the other hand it appears that workers are reluctant to offer their services at less than the prevailing rates when the demand for labour is low and unemployment is high so that wage rates fall only very slowly. The relationship between unemployment and the rate of change of wage rates is therefore likely to be non-linear. (Phillips, 1958, p. 283)

The loops were explained as the consequence of a difference between years of rising business activity and years of decline. For example, at a 3 per cent unemployment rate the average experience would be a 1.2 per cent rate of change in money wages; but this would be the average of a higher rate (in a period of growth) and a lower rate (when the economy is heading towards a slump).

Phillips emphasised the tentative nature of these conclusions and indicated the 'need for much more detailed research into the relations between unemployment, wage rates, prices and productivity' (ibid., p. 289). That this was so and that Phillips's paper became the most frequently cited in the economics literature is testimony to its impact upon the study of macroeconomics. Phillips's recognition of the relevance of microeconomic principles – the role of the price mechanism in a dynamic labour market – became the prominent feature of subsequent research. This gave emphasis to labour turnover and its associated frictional unemployment, as individual workers search the job market to assess the merits of alternative job offers.

THE EXPECTATIONS-AUGMENTED PHILLIPS CURVE

Theoretical variations and different statistical procedures were employed to augment the orginal version of Phillips's curve. Where data could be found, research economists rushed in with their novel propositions. Many contributions were made, but the most revealing theoretical developments were those which linked Phillips's work to monetary theory. In particular, Milton Friedman and Edmund Phelps (see Friedman, 1968 and Phelps, 1968) separately produced a framework which not only accommodated the evidence of a robust relationship between money wage changes and the level of unemployment (that is, the Phillips curve), but also accounted for the breakdown of the relationship during inflationary periods (such as the common experience of western economies from the late 1960s).

A distinction was drawn. First, there were periods of monetary stability, when price rises in one period (boom) were expected to be cancelled by price reductions in another (slump). (These were the basis for Phillips's fitted curves.) Business and labour came to know and to accept this continuing pattern. By contrast, a quite different experience – where prices have risen, are rising, and are expected to continue to rise – causes both business and labour to react quite differently.

With particular regard to the jobs market, a money wage offer would be assessed rather differently where next period's prices are expected to be higher (and then to rise still higher) than those currently prevailing.

Consider an individual looking for work. Various characteristics will be attached to unfilled vacancies; but abstracting from non-pecuniary considerations, a job seeker will have specific wage aspirations. For example, an individual may initially be interested in offers of no less than the wage received in his last job; or, alternatively, welfare benefits may set the lower limit to acceptable wage offers. The Friedman–Phelps argument is that job seekers set this limit – the *reservation wage* – in real terms; that is, in terms of the anticipated purchasing power of the money wage offer.

The original stable Phillips curve illustrated an inverse association between percentage money wage increases and the unemployment rate during non-inflationary periods. In boom and slump prices rose and fell to the same degree, while the trend of money wages was in line with the rate of increase in labour productivity. In such circumstances, labour turnover produces the frictional unemployment which always exists in a dynamic economy. This has come to be known as the 'natural rate of unemployment'; that is, that amount of unemployment associated with the absence of unanticipated price inflation.

By contrast, where persistent price rises have been the experience, workers will have discovered the disappointment of having the value of money wage increases eroded by price increases. Future price levels will then be anticipated and account taken of those expectations in setting the reservation wage. Thereby, the Phillips curve relationship between the rate of increase in money wages and the percentage rate of unemployment must be affected: to accommodate the 'cost of living' component in money wage offers, the curve must shift outwards. For, at any given rate of unemployment, the rate of increase in money wages will be that much greater.

To those who had interpreted the original Phillips curve as promising a permanent trade-off between inflation and unemployment, the experience of stagflation – the coincidence of high inflation and high unemployment – in the 1970s, came as a heavy blow. Increasingly, it became clear that full employment was not to be bought with monetary expansion.

THE INTERDEPENDENCE OF MONETARY AND FISCAL POLICY

In bringing together the topics of money, prices, wages and employment, Monetarism called into question the relevance of fiscal expansion as the means to reduce unemployment. Keynesianism, as it was developed after Keynes, had given too little attention to the monetary consequences of fiscal expansion.

The (public sector) budgetary stance is represented by the difference between government expenditure (G) and tax revenue (T), which gives the public sector borrowing requirement ($PSBR$):

$$G - T = PSBR \qquad (4)$$

Fiscal expansion necessarily causes the $PSBR$ to rise. This may have direct implications for the money supply; for that part of the $PSBR$ which is *not* raised from 'the market' (that is, in the same way as a large business corporation raises loans, by offering sufficiently attractive terms to potential lenders) must be met by the central bank (that is, by printing money). Thus, in any given period, the change in the money supply (ΔM) will be equal to that part of the $PSBR$ which is not raised from the market ($PSBR - \Delta GBP$), plus new commercial bank lending to the private sector (ΔPBB):

$$\Delta M = PSBR - \Delta GBP + \Delta PBB \qquad (5)$$

where

ΔGBP = any increase in government borrowing from the non-bank private sector (that is, from the market)
ΔPBB = any increase in bank lending to the private sector.

The interdependence of monetary policy and fiscal policy (and credit policy and interest rate policy, if they are to be afforded separate distinction) may be understood on the basis of equation (5).

(i) Monetary policy represents the government's position in exercising control over the money supply. Changes in the money supply appear on the left side of equation (5).
(ii) Fiscal policy determines the balance between government expenditure and receipts from tax revenue; this balance determines the magnitude of the budget deficit and hence the *PSBR*.
(iii) Interest rate policy reflects government concern with the cost of borrowing. The extent to which the government raises new loans in competition with others (ΔGBP), has a direct bearing upon interest rates. The more that the government attempts to borrow from this source, the higher interest rates will be driven.
(iv) Credit policy gives expression to the government's desire to exercise control over the net additional credit extended by the banking system to private sector borrowers (ΔPBB).

Thus the four strands of budgetary policy are shown to be interdependent. Even were the government able to achieve a precise control, it would be free to determine only three of the four strands. To illustrate, if the levels of government expenditure and likely tax revenues are given, then the *PSBR* is determined; if the government then decides to limit commercial bank advances to private borrowers (ΔPBB), its remaining option would lie between setting *either* the level for the change in the money supply (ΔM), *or* the level for government borrowing from the non-bank private sector (ΔGBP). If the decision is taken to limit the latter, then ΔM will find its own level. If the government decides to control the former, then interest rates will find their own level.

In summary, the logic of budgetary policy affords three degrees of freedom within the four policy options. All permutations of three from four are possible.

Beyond this tautological interrelationship, the outcome of policy will be affected by the behaviour of economic agents in reacting to changes in policy. Suppose, for example, that policy determines the magnitudes of ΔM and the PSBR. It follows from equation (5) that the aggregate value ($\Delta PBB - \Delta GBP$) is thereby determined. So, having chosen to control ΔM, the government cannot determine the level of interest rates, where both ΔPBB and ΔGBP are influential. So what might happen?

Suppose the set values of ΔM and the PSBR cause an initial sharp rise in interest rates. Then, two alternative behavioural reactions show quite different outcomes for the effects of policy:

(a) the demand for new bank credit (ΔPBB) might fall, in which case the amount of new net borrowing from the non-bank private sector (ΔGBP) would have to be reduced (to be consistent with the set values of ΔM and PSBR). Furthermore, given the composition of the PSBR (see Appendix equation A2), it would be necessary to offset the reduction in ΔGBP by an increase in either government bank borrowing (ΔGBB) or the issue of new cash ($\Delta PC + \Delta BC$), or both. All in all, this would serve to check the initial sharp rise in interest rates.

(b) the demand for new bank credit might rise as, unable either to repay the principal or to meet the higher charges, private sector borrowers negotiate with the banks to allow their outstanding debts to increase *pro rata* with the increase in interest charges. Then, ΔPBB would increase, and ΔGBP would have to be increased (to be consistent with the set values of ΔM and PSBR). Furthermore (by equation A2), it would be necessary to offset the increase in ΔGBP by a reduction in either government bank borrowing (ΔGBB) or the withdrawal of cash ($\Delta PC + \Delta BC$), or both. All in all, this would give further stimulus to the initial sharp rise in interest rates.

It is arguable that whereas alternative (b) describes the most likely *immediate* reaction on the part of existing borrowers, potential new borrowers would be deterred by higher interest charges, so that alternative (a) would become the dominant effect with the passing of time. At any point of time, the precise balance between opposing behavioural patterns cannot be established *a priori*; and so the implications for short-term forecasting are rather obvious. This is reflected in eleven central propositions of Monetarism (see Friedman, 1970, p. 22).

MONETARISM: THE CENTRAL PROPOSITIONS

1. A consistent, though not precise, relationship exists between growth in the money supply and growth in nominal income.
2. It takes time for monetary growth to affect income.
3. A change in the rate of monetary growth affects the rate of growth of nominal income with a time lag of between six to nine months.
4. A change in the growth of nominal income shows first in real output and hardly at all in prices.
5. The effect on prices occurs about six months after the effect on nominal income, so the total delay between a change in monetary growth and a change in the rate of inflation is between twelve to eighteen months.
6. Even allowing for time lags, the relationship is far from perfect.
7. In the short term, which may be as much as five to ten years, monetary changes mainly affect output. Over decades, monetary changes only affect prices; while output remains unaffected since, in the long run, output depends only upon real factors such as enterprise, ingenuity and thrift.
8. 'Inflation is always and everywhere a monetary phenomenon.'
9. Government spending may or may not be inflationary. It will be inflationary if it is financed by creating money, that is, by printing currency or creating bank deposits.
10. An increase in the rate of monetary growth raises the amount of cash which must be held in relation to other assets. With the attempt to reduce cash balances, there is a tendency for asset prices to increase and for interest rates to fall. This encourages expenditure upon the production of new assets. It also encourages spending on current services rather than upon existing assets. So the initial impact upon balance sheets is translated into an effect upon income and spending.
11. Monetary expansion initially lowers interest rates but, as spending and price inflation increase, it also produces a rise in the demand for loans which tends eventually to raise interest rates. This explains why Monetarists insist that interest rates are a highly misleading guide to monetary policy. Moreover, rising (or falling) prices introduce a discrepancy between real and nominal interest rates which disturbs real sectors of the economy.

8 Control of the Money Supply

> The only way to avoid being driven by continuing inflation into a controlled and directed economy, and therefore ultimately in order to save civilisation, will be to deprive governments of their power over the supply of money. (Hayek, 1978, p. 129)

The Monetarist view is that the four strands of budgetary policy – monetary, fiscal, interest rate and credit policy – ought not to be regarded as a basis for manipulating the behaviour of economic agents. The argument is that microeconomic principles show the effectiveness of market forces in achieving an efficient allocation of resources; and that these considerations are not compromised by any wider consideration, macroeconomic in kind. In particular, Friedman has argued that by seeking to keep monetary disturbances to a minimum,

> steady monetary growth would provide a monetary climate favourable to the effective operation of those basic forces of enterprise, ingenuity, invention, hard work and thrift that are the true springs of economic growth. (Friedman, 1968, p. 17)

How is this to be achieved?

Equation (5) in Chapter 7 encompasses the nature of the objective: to control the money supply, the government must control

(a) that part of its own borrowing raised from the banking sector.
(b) the amount of private sector borrowing from the banking sector.

PUBLIC SECTOR BANK BORROWING

Why should the government choose to borrow at all when it has the authority to raise taxes? The most telling argument is that taxation entails compulsion and is unpopular. By contrast, a loan raised against competition in financial markets represents a contract freely entered into. (Although there is no free volition with respect to the obligation of future generations of taxpayers to repay those loans.) In borrowing openly from the market, the government must accept interest rates set by the forces of supply and demand. The more it seeks to borrow, the higher rates of interest will be driven. Not only does this raise the cost of government borrowing, but high interest rates themselves are unpopular. The government faces a clear temptation to borrow from the banking sector.

When it raises a loan from its central bank, the government competes with no other borrower. Unlike a loan to the government raised from the market, a loan from its bank represents no transfer of real resources. It is a purely bookkeeping transaction whereby the bank acquires government debt (a bank asset) in return for which it creates a deposit in the name of the government (a bank liability). Thus, the government acquires new spending power without causing interest rates to rise. Nevertheless, the attractiveness of this source of funds is largely illusory.

At the stage where the government obtains its loan from the central bank, there is no impact upon the economy. The bank has the government's receipt (in the usual form of interest-bearing stock) as part of its portfolio of assets, and stands ready to honour cheques drawn against the government's new deposit. This is pure bookkeeping. Only when the government begins to draw upon its new account do other parties become involved.

Suppose, for example, the government writes cheques to pay its civil servants. These are deposited with commercial banks where, by definition, they form part of the money supply (see Appendix). So, given that bank borrowing by the government causes the money supply to increase, why should not more direct use be made of the printing press to produce new money to finance expenditure? Would this not be less costly than raising revenue by issuing interest-bearing stock? Such a conclusion would be premature.

To continue with the illustration: the cheques, which the commercial banks receive as new deposits, constitute highly liquid non-interest-bearing assets. These must change the composition of the banks' portfolio of assets, and readjustment is to be expected. For example, the cheques might be used to acquire interest-bearing government stock; that is, that same stock which was acquired initially by the government's own central bank to secure the original loan to the government.

Clearly, the manner in which government revenue is raised has implications for the liquidity requirements of the banking system at large. For example, commercial banks might be left with *either* an excess proportion of interest-bearing stock (in the case of new government borrowing), *or* an excessive proportion of notes and coins (in the case of new note printing). With the latter, excessive balances of notes and coins would be used to buy government stock. This would cause stock prices to rise and interest rates to fall. With the former, commercial banks would sell stock, which would cause stock prices to fall and interest rates to rise.

The government cannot be indifferent to repercussions of this kind, not least because it is mindful of the implications for the burden of interest payments upon outstanding debt, and of the effect upon future sales of government stock. So the choice between raising money by way of the printing press, or by selling new stock to the banking sector, is by no means free of constraints.

Nevertheless, either means would cause the money supply to increase by the exact same amount. Subsequently, even this increase would be magnified by the bank credit multiplier as commercial banks are able to extend credit upon the basis of the new reserve assets received; for, not only notes and coin, but short-dated government stock would be regarded as secure reserve assets against which bank credit creation could be extended.

PRIVATE SECTOR BANK BORROWING

That part of any change in the money supply which is most obviously within the influence of the government was shown by equation (5) in Chapter 7 to be the difference between the government's own required level of borrowing (*PSBR*) and that amount which it borrows from the non-bank private sector (ΔGBP). In sketching the consequences of alternative strategies for public sector borrowing, the arguments came naturally to the question of the further stimulus which new reserve assets would give to bank credit creation. This is the other component of any change in the money supply as shown by equation (5) in Chapter 7; that is, the change in bank lending to the private sector (ΔPBB).

Credit is the indebtedness of one individual or institution to another and so there is no reliance of credit upon the existence of banks; but bank involvement changes the nature of credit, for credit becomes money whenever the outstanding liability itself becomes acceptable as a medium of exchange. The extension of credit by banks creates money because, for all practicable purposes, a cheque drawn upon a bank account is an acceptable medium of exchange.

The degree to which government can exercise control over the extension of bank credit depends upon the amount of reserve assets held by the banks (that is, the 'monetary base') upon which the extension of credit is based. For the government to be able to exercise control over bank loans to the private sector, it must establish effective control over the whole process of bank credit creation. This would require the following:

(a) a precise definition of those assets which are eligible as reserve assets;
(b) close control over the issue of reserve assets;
(c) a minimum ratio of reserve assets to total assets;
(d) close surveillance of banking practice.

With such conditions, it is argued that governments would be able to control the aggregate level of private borrowing from a financial system in which banking practice would have become highly formalised and tightly controlled. A contrary view is that controls of this kind would provide the incentive for the creation of new kinds of financial intermediaries, offering credit arrangements to evade controls established by the authorities over *bona fide* banking institutions. In modern jargon, these are the arguments for and against 'monetary base control'; but the arguments are not new. They are the resurrection of a controversy which began a century earlier, and which may be most readily understood within that historical context.

BANKING SCHOOL VERSUS CURRENCY SCHOOL

In the mid-nineteenth century, there were two views relating to note issue. The Currency School held that a mixed gold-paper currency should be so regulated as to ensure that it behaved like a purely metallic commodity. The objective was to maintain the gold convertibility of sterling (equivalent to the modern objective of limiting the monetary base to achieve effective control over money and prices).

The Banking School countered with the argument that statutory control of currency is unnecessary so long as convertibility is maintained. Moreover, the use of bank deposits, bills of exchange, and other substitutes for bank notes would defeat any such attempts at control. The Banking School took the view that the note issue *responded* to the price level.

Support was drawn from statistical evidence – Thomas Tooke's study of the period from 1792 to 1856[1] – and from an understanding of central banking practice. Tooke showed that, in the early phases of any boom, the London money market readily provided loans, leaving the Bank of England as a bystander. As the boom continued, commodity prices rose and credit became harder to obtain. Increasingly, traders were forced to borrow from the Bank of England at its high penal Bank Rate. As a direct consequence, the Bank's note issue increased – but this was *after* the increase in prices.

From these observations it was argued that the Currency School was wrong to claim that excessive note issue was the *cause* of price inflation, commercial crises, and the threat to convertibility. An essential ingredient, in the Banking School's critique of the Currency School, was that control over the Bank of England's note issue would *not* establish control over credit. Supporters of the currency principle countered that, while credit could influence prices just as much as notes and coins, the latter provided the monetary base and would remain the preferred instrument for final payment.

The Banking School favoured less regulation of banks, believing that the note issue should not be the sole prerogative of the state. It was argued that the provision of bank credit could never be extended beyond the 'needs-of-trade'. If ever it were attempted, the 'law of reflux' would operate with the effect that excess money balances would be returned to the banks as repayments of loans.

In modern debate, the law of reflux has been revived as part of the Keynesian counter-attack upon Monetarism. As before, the argument is that the extension of bank credit is constrained by the needs of trade because 'an excess supply of credit money can be reduced simply through the repayment of bank credit' (Bootle, 1984, p. 4).[2] To illustrate, suppose that the supply of bank credit were suddenly increased as all banks (through a deliberate change in policy) agreed to finance more risky ventures. The expenditure financed by this new credit would certainly give new income recipients the opportunity to pay off their own overdrawn accounts; and if they were to do so, the Banking School's case would be confirmed. It is not the logic of the law of reflux which is questioned, but its relevance.

The alternative scenario is that additional money income generated by the expenditure of new bank credit would be used to finance still more expenditure. Higher money incomes would give recipients the opportunity to expand their trading; that is, 'the needs of trade' would not be a static constraint. Monetary expansion would *cause* prices to rise, thereby giving rise to an increase in the public's demand to hold money. Equilibrium in money markets would be eventually re-established at higher levels of nominal money prices and incomes.

MONEY SUBSTITUTES AND THE CONTROL OF MONEY

In support of Banking School principles, recent evidence has been interpreted to indicate that empirical links between money and prices exist only for periods when the authorities have made no attempt to manipulate money aggregates as instruments of policy. Where limits have been applied to the growth of money, it is argued that it has been relatively easy for the community to switch to available substitutes which are not subject to control. This view is now enshrined as Goodhart's Law 'that *any* observed regularity will tend to collapse once pressure is placed upon it for control purposes' (Goodhart, 1984, p. 96), according to which any definition of money must lose all relevance once it becomes the target for official control.

The history of financiers' initiative and inventiveness lends plausibility to the argument that non-bank financial intermediaries can thwart attempts at monetary base control. That such developments would be forthcoming is scarcely in doubt, but so too is the conclusion that these would frustrate the attempt to control the level of private sector borrowing. Unlike the many historical examples of quantitative controls – rationing in various forms – the proposals for monetary base control represent a call for the application of the well-tried market mechanism.

By setting the required minimum ratio of reserve assets (to bank liabilities) at a level close to the operational standards established by sound banking practice, the government could ensure that banks would be affected by any decision to restrict the supply of those *bona fide* assets (often termed 'high-powered money'). Such action would force commercial banks to curtail their extension of credit to the private sector. Disappointed prospective borrowers would be forced to look elsewhere, to alternative sources of credit. Inventiveness would ensure the availabilty of such credit, but at a price. The very fact that these new institutions are unable to compete *before* the contraction of the supply of reserve assets implies that they are higher cost alternatives.

Even if banks were totally unrestricted by regulations, so that they were permitted to operate at any ratio of reserve assets, leverage could still be exercised by the method chosen to finance the *PSBR*. This would determine the amount of *bona fide* (though no longer in any legal sense) assets released into circulation. Such a regime might be expected to bring less conservative financial practices, more spectacular successes, and more disastrous failures. It would also lead financial analysts to create an even greater confusion (than at present) of statistical measures of *the* aggregate money supply; but none of this should obscure the mechanism by which the government has the power to determine the level, and to cause changes in the level, of money and prices.

The abolition of statutory reserve requirements certainly raises the possibility of the large-scale substitution of interest-bearing assets for non-interest-bearing money. Whereas Friedman has endorsed reform along these lines, he argues for a cautious approach (see Friedman, 1987, p. 377). The first stage would be to freeze the growth of high-powered money; followed later by the elimination of reserve requirements and other regulations. Zero growth of high-powered money has a special appeal in that it would prove harder to talk the rate up on political grounds: 'as a psychological matter' zero has a qualitative difference from, say, rates of 2 or 3 per cent.

On past trends of rising velocity of circulation, such a target rate would be consistent with the liquidity needs of a growing economy. Moreover, the process of deregulation and innovation within financial markets would suggest a further steady rise of the money multiplier, to ensure the compatibility of price stability with the zero growth of high-powered money. In coming to this position, Friedman acknowledges the influence of Hayek; but while Friedman has been guided by detailed empirical analysis conducted over many years, Hayek's advocacy of a fully competitive financial system is grounded upon the ideology of liberalism.

HAYEK AND THE REJECTION OF MONETARY POLICY

While there is little doubt that monetary control, exercised by the state, could be made effective, Hayek has questioned whether governments can be trusted to act dispassionately: 'A good money, like a good law, must operate without regard to the effect that decisions of the issuer will have on known groups of individuals' (Hayek, 1978, p. 113). When Keynesian economists began to advise finance ministers that a budget deficit was a meritorious act, persistent inflation became inevitable. While some have recognised the harmful consequences, the temptation to adopt practices with an inflationary impact is ever present. As a counterpoise and politically feasible first step, other bodies (for example, the monetary authorities of other nations) might be allowed to compete with the domestic provision of money assets. Then individuals would be able to exercise consumer sovereignty over money, as with other goods sold in open competition.

To this end, Hayek has proposed that the free nations of the world should

> mutually bind themselves by formal treaty not to place any obstacles in the way of free dealing throughout their territories in one another's currencies, or of similar free exercise of banking business. (Hayek, 1978, p. 19)

If this proposal were adopted, it would be impossible for any national authority to issue money in any way inferior to that of any other nation. Any deviation from the path of providing sound money would lead rapidly to the displacement of the offending country's currency.

That bank deregulation is consistent with the monetary discipline necessary to preclude inflation might appear odd. If so, then it arises from the association of discipline with monolithic institutional authority. There is another kind; that imposed by the impartial interplay of market forces. For Hayek, the felt need to define, monitor, and to regulate is an anathema, and this applies to money as to all things else. It is an idea which can be traced to *The Wealth of Nations*, where 'Smith maintained that, even for the money supply, the operation of market forces could and should be relied upon as confidently as for the wine supply' (Hutchinson, 1980, p. 4). According to this view, the only sure safeguard against the harmful abuse of monopoly power (over money) by government is the denationalisation of money.

Monopolisation of the note issue by the central authorities operates as an effective constraint upon competition. Although money substitutes abound, they are inextricably bound to the official note issue by legal tender provisions. Competition between private issuers would force each to regulate the supply of his own currency so as to ensure its continuing acceptability. The expansion of new currencies would reduce the demand for existing state currencies and – unless their volume were to be rapidly decreased – lead to their depreciation in value. By this same process, all unreliable currencies would eventually be eliminated.

While these objectives are in keeping with the spirit of Monetarism, Hayek is critical of the idea that there could ever be any such quantity as *the* money supply. With the variety of alternative highly liquid assets available, attempts to delineate and to control any specific subset is meaningless in terms of its impact upon the volume of highly liquid assets in circulation. Hayek is, therefore, dismissive of the 'Monetarist Rule' to keep constant the rate of change in the total quantity of money (however defined). Rather,

> It demands something similar yet significantly different, namely that the quantity of money (or rather the aggregate of all the most liquid assets) be kept such that people will not reduce or increase their outlay for the purpose of adapting their balances to their altered liquidity preferences. (Hayek, 1978, p. 77)

But this must be left to market forces, for 'No authority can beforehand ascertain, and only the market can discover, the 'optimal quantity of money' (ibid.).

9 International Trade and Exchange Rate Policy

> There are strong presumptions of a general character against trade restrictions unless they can be justified on special grounds. (Keynes, 1936, p. 338)

How is it that trade takes place within national boundaries without attracting the attention given to international transactions? Why is it that governments insist upon supervision, documentation and detailed analysis of the latter, while leaving domestic trade unencumbered? After all, the geographical division of the world into sovereign states is of no relevance to those principles which determine the efficiency of the market process in allocating resources.

Monetary theory provides one explanation. Holders of state token money provide the state with an interest-free loan. While the volume of domestic trade has no direct impact upon the amount of token money in circulation, this is not the case with foreign trade. State token money is only acceptable to overseas suppliers when it can be exchanged for state money of their own country. A certain reluctance on the part of the importing state can be imagined.

When the state exchanges gold or foreign currency reserves for domestic tokens, its interest-free borrowing is directly reduced. Transactions in the opposite direction increase gold and foreign currency reserves. So, within the limited perspective of raising state finance, it is possible to understand the asymmetrical view of foreign trade, that exports are desirable and imports undesirable. It is a view with antecedents reaching back to the fourteenth century. Subsequently:

> The notion that bullion supplied 'the sinews of war' had genuine appeal in the days of Henry VIII, and when Henry squandered the state treasure this idea persisted, fed by rational fear of liquidity in an era when credit institutions were little developed. (Blaug, 1978, p. 18)

From the sixteenth through to the mid-eighteenth century, support grew for the 'balance of trade doctrine'; and the thesis that a trade surplus was desirable became known as mercantilism. It is an idea which has presented a recurring theme through to the present day.

MERCANTILISM

The mercantilist view is that national welfare is enhanced by a trade surplus. It provides the bullion necessary to support the international power of the state; but a trade surplus is also good for commerce. This derives from the idea that the volume of world resources is finite, so that nations must compete for a prize of fixed dimensions. A nation prospers only at the expense of other nations. In short, the mercantilist philosophy is the antithesis of belief in the *mutual* gains from trade.

That exports are a net addition to sales in the home market and that imports are a threat to employment and production in domestic trades is a view with popular appeal. However, sound economic analysis runs counter to intuition. Nineteenth-century utilitarian analysis demonstrated the mutual gains from free trade; but there was a much earlier recognition of the logical impossibility of the mercantilist objective: 'Thomas Munn, writing as early as 1630, had realised that an inflow of bullion raises domestic prices and that "selling dear and buying cheap" turns the balance of trade against a country' (ibid. p. 13). The crux of this early counter to mercantilism lay with the 'specie flow mechanism' whereby commodity money (gold specie) was used to finance international transactions. With a trade surplus there is a net inflow of specie which enters either directly into domestic circulation as commodity money or else is converted into state token money. Either way, there is an increase in the quantity of money in circulation in the trade surplus nation. According to the Quantity Theory of money, this causes domestic prices to rise. Similarly, but in reverse sequence, a nation with a trade deficit experiences falling prices.

With the pattern of international trade responding to changes in relative prices, the surplus nation finds it increasingly difficult to sell its goods abroad, while the deficit nation finds it increasingly easy. So is established a natural mechanism – the specie flow mechanism – which must inhibit the mercantilist objective of persistent trade surpluses. Although the flow of gold specie was superseded by more efficient instruments, the principle by which adjustment takes place remained unaffected by these new developments.

THE GOLD BULLION STANDARD

The use of gold specie to pay for foreign goods gave way to the gold bullion standard. More manageable and of greater uniformity than specie, gold bullion became the ultimate standard of value of state currencies. In the nineteenth century, a trading nation stood ready to redeem a unit of its own token money with a fixed weight of gold. For any two 'convertible' currencies, this mechanism established a fixed rate of exchange – the price of one currency in units of the other.

If the UK were to run a trade deficit there would be an excess supply of sterling on foreign exchange markets (more sterling would be used to pay for UK imports than the amount required to buy UK exports). As the excess supply of sterling begins to depress the sterling exchange rate below the official rate given by the gold bullion standard, the Bank of England must buy sterling with gold. Were this not to happen, the sterling exchange rate would continue to fall, and a point would be reached where UK importers would cease to pay the high price for foreign currency and (notwithstanding the extra cost of shipping bullion) would find it cheaper to buy gold bullion from the Bank of England for shipment overseas.

The outflow of bullion to pay for imports would reduce the money supply. (Sterling notes acquired by the Bank of England from the sale of bullion do not form part of the domestic money supply – those notes are the Bank's IOUs to itself.) Prices would fall. UK goods would become relatively more attractive to foreign customers, and the downward pressure upon the sterling exchange rate would cease.

The historical record shows that international shipments of bullion were small when set against the size of trade deficits. Also, nothing like a proportional relationship existed between the outflow of gold bullion and the level of domestic prices. However, these should not be interpreted as evidence against the automatic adjustment mechanism. There were a number of explanations:

(a) borrowing: by raising interest rates, a nation with a trade deficit can attract funds from overseas. (Loans from abroad are synonymous with capital exports.) This creates an additional demand for the domestic currency to offset the excess supply arising from the trade deficit. Capital exports are an alternative to gold bullion exports.
(b) falling incomes: where a trade deficit is attributable to some natural catastrophe (such as harvest failure), the loss of (farm) income reduces the demand for imported goods. Reductions in domestic

incomes are an alternative to gold bullion exports.
(c) gold substitutes: although debased, coins were generally accepted at their fiat value in everyday transactions (see Gould, 1970, p. 17), but with larger international transactions these coins were handled only at a discount. Currency debasement broke the linkage between gold outflows and changes in the domestic money supply.
(d) reserve banking: where gold is the reserve asset for bank credit creation, a small change in gold reserves leads to a multiple contraction of the domestic money supply. Bank credit contraction is an alternative to gold bullion exports. Reserve banking broke the linkage between gold outflows and changes in the domestic money supply.

By whichever combination of adjustments a trade imbalance is accommodated, the essential feature is that the adjustment mechanism operates *automatically*; that is, it requires no discretionary intervention by state authorities to maintain currency convertibilty.

THE GOLD-EXCHANGE STANDARD

The gold bullion standard was an early casualty of the First World War. This was no surprise. War radically alters patterns of trade and finance. International payments obligations are either repudiated or deferred. The domestic suspension of currency convertibility is also a common feature as governments anticipate a greater inclination to hoard gold during periods of great uncertainty. Forcible substitution of paper for gold has a number of advantages for a state at war.

The removal of gold from circulation may impede black market trade. Furthermore, state custody of domestic holdings of gold precludes hoarding with its implications for domestic trade. Paper notes provide the same purchasing power as gold, but are discounted as a long term security. Any tendency to hoard paper currency would be offset (and deterred) by active use of the printing press. In any case, wartime controls, rationing, and the obligation to accept legal tender all run counter to the money economy.

With peace, there was widespread agreement in the West that a restored gold standard was a first requirement for long-term economic stability; but it was evident that the totality of gold was insufficient to maintain the convertibility of currencies at existing price levels. The solution of raising the price of gold was not pursued.

Instead, by a resolution of a conference held at Genoa in 1922, it was recommended that economy in the use of gold might be achieved 'by maintaining reserves in the form of foreign balances'. In its implementation, this recommendation saw the inauguration of the gold-exchange standard which, although it was forced into abeyance during the Great Depression, was to be fully restored at Bretton Woods in 1944.

Insobriety and head-pain are positively correlated. Positive, too, is the relationship between the ease with which it is possible to restore gold as the standard of value and earlier monetary profligacy. It is never a costless exercise. For the UK, in the early 1920s, restoration of full currency convertibility (at the pre-war dollar/sterling rate of exchange) was adopted as a policy objective. To this end, a package of deflationary measures was introduced and sustained, but it achieved only temporary success. Despite the costs in terms of lost trade and unemployment, the restoration of the gold convertibility in 1925 was dashed by the financial collapse of the New York Stock Exchange four years later.

Offended by the excesses of vacuous business ventures and speculative finance, governments were guided by their most conservative instincts. Deflation and real economic distress were the universal experience. There was no easy solution. Rather, international trade was much inhibited by the resurgence of mercantilist obsessions with national gold stocks. Through the 1930s, international trade and capital mobility were heavily constrained by government controls.

Although the Second World War was hugely destructive of wealth and productive potential, positive institutional reform neutralised the mercantilist obsession. At Bretton Woods in 1944, representatives of western nations agreed to a regime of fixed exchange rates, within which the US dollar replaced gold as the international reserve asset. Currencies were convertible into the dollar, and the dollar was convertible into gold. Thereby the gold exchange standard was re-created.

By the principles of this system, central banks were permitted to extend credit upon the basis of reserves of other convertible currencies. Thus, a nation having a trade surplus with the USA would accept interest-bearing dollar securities (rather than gold). Like gold these would form part of the reserve base of the domestic trading system; but (unlike gold) these assets would remain in the USA where, there too, they would continue to be used as a basis for the extension of bank credit:

The international monetary system thus came to resemble a group of children playing marbles who agree that after each game the losers would get back the marbles they have put up. (Rueff, 1964, p. 117)

The Bretton Woods system was created in preference to Keynes's proposals for an international reserve currency based upon assets pooled by participating central banks. Ironically, the principal reason for rejection was their alleged inflationary bias. Certainly, Keynes had been critical of the old gold standard for attributes which Hayek had considered to be its merits (see Hayek, 1943, p. 176); that is, that monetary policy would be determined by non-domestic considerations. Keynes had argued that the degree to which price stability would prove commensurate with full employment would differ between nations. If wages and credit policy moved out of step, exchange rate adjustment was preferable to recurrent periods of unemployment which, until then, had been 'the only effective means of holding efficiency wages within a reasonably stable range' (Keynes, 1943, p. 186). Yet, given the commitment to high aggregate demand, Keynes gave no suggestions for control of domestic wages and prices.

With hindsight it is clear that the Bretton Woods arrangements provided insufficient discipline. Two escape clauses were given too much prominence. Credit was available from the newly formed International Monetary Fund; and there was easy access for nations which persistently absorbed resources beyond their ability to pay. Secondly, exchange rate readjustment allowed monetary expansion to continue unchecked. Most importantly, the monetary profligacy of US budgets in the late 1960s produced a glut of paper reserves which threatened convertibility and the international reserve currency status of the US dollar.

EXCHANGE RATES IN THE POST-1945 PERIOD

Under the Bretton Woods agreement, a revaluation of a currency was permitted whenever there arose a 'fundamental disequilibrium' in a nation's balance of payments. Although this condition was never given a precise definition, it was understood to exist whenever the balance for official financing was both persistent and large in relation to gold and foreign exchange reserves.

This situation was likely to arise whenever the automatic mechanism of internal price adjustment, by which the gold bullion standard formerly operated, was impeded by other forces. For example, deliberate monetary expansion by a deficit nation could offset the contraction in the money supply resulting from the trade deficit; and political expediency frequently led to this outcome. In this, deficit nations faced little discouragement, for the Bretton Woods agreement placed the burden of adjustment largely upon surplus nations. Thus were created the foundations for world inflation in which Keynes had exerted significant influence:

> It was an essential part of the Keynes plan that the responsibility of relative adjustment, where the existing exchange rate and price relations did not provide a basis for equilibrium, should be laid on creditors as well as debtors, so that the pressure on the debtor to deflate and contract income should be mitigated. (Robinson, 1947, pp. 54–5)

Many realignments took place. Two involved sterling. The first, in 1949, was the result of the restoration of convertibility at an overvalued rate. The second, in 1967, was an early sign that western nations were about to be shaken from the Keynesian dream of high levels of public expenditure without soundly based finance. This devaluation was a deliberate attempt to tackle the problem of chronic trade deficits, which had so plagued the commitment to full employment levels of aggregate demand; but it failed in its objective because it was applied as an *alternative* to a lower standard of living, rather than as the means to achieving that end.

During the early phase of post-war reconstruction, it had suited others for the USA to run trade deficits: these had increased the volume of dollars which other nations had been glad to seize upon. Dollars were near to gold. Cautious fiscal policies had sustained the dominant position of the dollar; but this had been ended by the Kennedy/Johnson commitment to social welfare expenditure at home, and to defence expenditure in south-east Asia.

The strength of the dollar began to wane as lax budgetary policies resulted not only in low interest rates, but also in surging balance of payments deficits. With low yields in the USA, dollars left in search of higher returns, while recurring current account deficits were financed by printing more dollars. Eventually, this rising supply was interpreted as a glut, and the erosion of confidence culminated in the suspension of dollar convertibility in August 1971. By mid-1973, the exchange rates of all major currencies were floating against each other.

THE BALANCE OF PAYMENTS ACCOUNTS

As with the modern practice of keeping national income accounts, the production of increasingly detailed balance of payments statistics was intended to provide the information upon which macroeconomic policy decisions might be based. This was especially relevant to the era of Keynesian demand management with its need for the effects of policy to be monitored in order that appropriate adjustments might be made. Of course, whether or not a particular set of accounts is viewed with dismay or delight turns on interpretation and the theory upon which that interpretation is based.

By the conventions of double-entry bookkeeping, the aggregate totals of transactions in foreign trade must necessarily balance. Individually, separate components will show positive or negative values, depending on whether net transactions in those particular categories are in surplus or deficit but, when all are taken together, these values must sum to zero. Payments must balance.

For a simple trading economy, the difference between exports and imports (the balance of trade) must be financed by the sale of gold bullion. For such an economy, the accounts would show

$$\text{balance of trade} + \text{gold flow} = 0 \qquad (1)$$

or, in modern jargon

$$\text{current account} + \text{capital account} = 0 \qquad (2)$$

A surplus on current account would be matched precisely by a deficit on capital account: an inflow of gold bullion is recorded as a net capital import.

In a slightly more sophisticated world, the current account would also comprise 'invisible' transactions; services of various kinds, banking, insurance, shipping and so on. Here the current account deficit measures the value of foreign goods and services purchased from abroad but not paid for out of current income from sales overseas. This deficit must be financed by capital exports.

Although any period in which there is a current account deficit shows the nation to be 'living beyond the means of its current income', this is not to argue that a current account deficit is bad, nor – as would fit the mercantilist philosophy – that a current account surplus is good. The precise nature of the accommodating values of capital account transactions would have to be judged before such conclusions are reached. Interpretations will vary.

Although mercantilism takes issue with a current account deficit, a more recent judgement is that long-term international capital movements give no cause for concern. If, for example, efficient work practices attract foreign investment into domestic capital projects, this is hardly indicative of a nation living beyond its current means. With considerations of this kind in mind, the 'basic balance' was coined, defined as the sum of the current account together with the net movement on the long-term capital account. If the basic balance were zero, there would be no cause for concern.

Another view is that the distinction between short-term and long-term capital movements is somewhat arbitrary; in which case so too is the definition of the basic balance. Rather, changes in official holdings of gold and foreign exchange reserves might warrant special attention. These, together with net foreign currency borrowing by the government, comprise the 'balance for official financing' which has been of greater interest to domestic authorities during periods when flexible exchange rates have operated. The balance for official financing is the amount which must either be met from (or absorbed by) official coffers if the exchange rate is to remain unchanged.

MONETARY THEORY OF THE BALANCE OF PAYMENTS

Preoccupation with currency exchange rates as the root cause of balance of payments problems may be traced to Bretton Woods. Fundamental truths of classical analysis were obscured by the drive for a planned post-war recovery of international trade and financial arrangements.

Notwithstanding the common experience of national and international bureaucratic structures, which impede the competitive process, the world economy is the market-place writ large. Where fixed exchange rates are administered by central banking authorities, an excess of domestic money supply (over the demand to hold money) shows itself in an excess domestic demand for commodities, which is met by imports. The trade deficit which results is necessarily balanced by payments in domestic currency. In the course of currency exchange, these produce a fall in foreign exchange reserves. By this act of exchange, currency is withdrawn from circulation.

In parallel with the specie flow adjustment mechanism of earlier trading arrangements, a reduction of the money supply is a central feature of international payments adjustments; and, with the re-emergence of the Quantity Theory, this monetary theory of balance of payments adjustment has experienced a revival.

More crucially, the important feature in this context is the recognition that, within a fixed exchange rate regime, any single nation finds it impossible to pursue an independent monetary policy. Fixed exchange rates effectively establish a world money supply with a single rate of aggregate growth. Attempts to establish a monetary regime which diverges from that world growth rate must lead to trade imbalance, money flows, and adjustments which bring the volume of money in circulation in line with the demand to hold money. In short, a balance of payments disequilibrium is a manifestation of monetary disequilibrium.

Although fixed exchange rates bring a degree of stability to international trade, this is achieved only at a superficial level. By forward exchange cover, or by pricing in a 'well-chosen' currency, any uncertainty arising from floating exchange rates can be reduced or eliminated. The great danger in relying upon a fixed exchange rate regime to bring greater certainty to trading arrangements is that its corollary is almost certain to be monetary instability; for by what criteria is the growth rate of the aggregate world money supply to be determined? International agreement here is a prerequisite of any scheme for fixed exchange rates (or even the more flexible schemes for 'exchange rate targeting').

EXCHANGE RATE TARGETING VERSUS MONETARY CONTROL

Many professional economists – the majority with Keynesian leanings – favour a return to a regime of fixed exchange rates which, they argue, offers advantages over the monetary targeting prescribed by Monetarism. This, despite the fact that central to the success of the Bretton Woods system was the extensive use of foreign exchange controls by participating nations.

Their belief is that a stable exchange rate brings greater stability to real sectors of the economy than constancy in monetary growth. There has to be this choice, because a given target for the exchange rate necessarily involves accommodating all desired sales/purchases of currencies at that rate. Much of their case rests upon the theoretical concept of 'exchange rate overshoot', which arises in the context of a macroeconomic model in which financial markets (dealing in money and assets, and responding to prices, exchange rates and interest rate differentials) respond quickly to any disturbances to equilibrium. By contrast, the goods market is assumed to respond much more slowly.

For illustration, consider the consequences of an equilibrium disturbed by an unanticipated contraction of the money supply. In the long term, this must lower the general level of prices and cause an appreciation of the exchange rate, while the impact upon the goods market would be neutral. More immediately, there would be a number of sequential repercussions. In financial markets, reacting with greatest speed, monetary contraction would lead to an increase in the rate of interest with implications (in the goods market) for investment expenditure and the structure of production, and (in the assets market, by creating a temporary gap between the domestic interest rate and world interest rate) for currency exchange rates.

Exchange rate overshoot occurs as part of the dynamic readjustment of financial and goods markets. It is assumed that the latter are slow to respond, so that, initially, output and real income remain unchanged; and so the demand for purchasing power (real balances) also remains unchanged. So the first consequences of monetary contraction are to be found in financial markets. Here the effects will be threefold:

(i) since monetary contraction will *ultimately* have the result of reducing prices in goods markets, efficient financial markets will incorporate *current* expectations of exchange rate *appreciation*;
(ii) in the period before prices fall, the *immediate* impact of monetary contraction will be to force up the domestic rate of interest, to a level above the world rate;
(iii) the domestic rate of interest can only lie above the world rate if there are *current* expectations of exchange rate *depreciation*. Otherwise, there would be an avalanche of foreign capital inflow.

The contradiction between (i) and (iii) is resolved by the operation of exchange rate overshoot. Effects (i) and (ii) will combine to attract an international capital inflow into the domestic economy. To accommodate effect (iii), this inflow must be large enough to cause an exchange rate appreciation of sufficient magnitude to *reverse* expectations; that is, there is an exchange rate overshoot which supports expectations of exchange rate *depreciation*.

Exchange rate overshoot is by no means inevitable. It relies upon differential rates of adjustment in different sectors of the economy. For example, to the extent that output *is* reduced as a consequence of monetary contraction, real incomes might be lowered sufficiently to reduce the demand for real balances in *greater* proportion to the original monetary contraction. This would result in an excess supply of liquidity which would push the domestic rate of interest *below* the world rate. Since this differential would require the expectation of exchange rate *appreciation*, there need be no overshoot.

Where financial markets cannot rely upon an assured regime of fixed exchange rates, judgements of current and expected future monetary policies of all the separate national authorities must continuously be formed. Each monetary authority has to accept that judgement and the implications for its own set of prices, rate of interest, exchange rate, income, output and employment. Yet, there remains a fear that the more rapid responses of financial markets might cause unwarranted costs of adjustment in the real sector of the economy: unwarranted because that adjustment eventually will have to be reversed (as when, following an exchange rate overshoot, there is a reversal towards the final equilibrium rate).

Faced by these possibilities, what operational rules should be adopted by a national monetary authority? According to Monetarism, pre-announced monetary targeting offers the greatest degree of stability to all sectors of the economy. The greater the success in meeting set targets, the more likely it is that exchange rate movements will represent reaction to pressure emanating from the real sector of the domestic economy.

In practice, many nations which have espoused pre-announced monetary targeting have relaxed those targets in response to 'unacceptable pressures' arising from exchange rate movements, where the recurring worry has been with costs borne by manufacturing sectors of the economy. In lay terms, the argument has been that of maintaining 'a competitive exchange rate'. Of course, although everyone knows what is meant by that term, there exists no definitional basis to identify where it is located!

From the Keynesian presumption that it is *always* beneficial for the authorities to retain the freedom to make discretionary adjustments to policy, the case has been made for a compromise (Artis and Currie, 1981 p. 193), that is, for 'conditionalising monetary targets on exchange rates', whereby upper and lower bounds are set for monetary growth. It is then argued that these constraints should be relaxed whenever currency market pressures threaten to broach these pre-set limits.

To repeat, this conclusion derives from the premise that it is better to keep the maximum number of options open, whence the deduction that it must be inappropriate for the authorities to adopt an inflexible 'no response' policy of pre-announced monetary targets. Use of such escape clauses must necessarily detract from the surety of domestic monetary stability; but, the relevant question is whether or not this would be offset by a 'less tipsy' trading sector which would then be in an improved position to deliver enhanced national economic welfare. This can only be resolved by the strength of argument or as a matter of faith.

Fixed exchange rates and the compromise of conditional monetary targets are both in opposition to the Monetarist Rule (of sticking to a monetary target) with its objective of removing discretionary adjustments, which are viewed as a *source* of disturbance to the real sectors of the economy. From Monetarism comes the fundamental objection to exchange rate targeting, which is that the exchange rate reflects the relative price of highly liquid financial assets. Although volume changes in the amount supplied of each currency are relevant to exchange rate movements, many other important determinants – including intangibles such as political uncertainty, business expectations, speculative rumours and so on – make it a practical nonsense for the authorities to regard the exchange rate as a reliable guide to changing economic conditions. In short, monetary policy cannot be based upon the multifarious 'alarms and excursions that affect exchange rates' (Walters, 1986, p. 133).

THE MYTH OF THE BALANCE OF PAYMENTS PROBLEM

There is a popular view that for the very 'open' UK economy, the balance of payments has been *the* economic problem, placing the most severe obstacle in the way of all that is economically good – high growth, low unemployment, and so on. Put simply, the argument is that those macroeconomic 'goods' are delivered by a high level of domestic aggregate demand, but that this causes a high demand for imports, wherein lies the problem.

Such an argument can be delivered with varying degrees of sophistication to reach the inevitable recommendation that free trade should be inhibited either directly by import controls or support for export industries, or indirectly by controlling international flows of capital. Always advocated and often implemented, these 'solutions' are in total contradiction of the view that national boundaries are inconsequential to the principles which determine efficient resource allocation.

Like any statistical record, balance of payments accounts can reflect symptoms of economic malaise. These should not be confused with the cause. To illustrate, most of the inhabitants of Wales live in blissful ignorance of the chronic deficit on the Welsh current account which – if they were kept – balance of payments accounts for Wales would show. This inference can be drawn from the fact that Wales is currently one of the depressed areas of the UK. The national uniformity of unemployment benefits and social security payments, together with the provision of public services and capital subsidies to industrial development, would be categorised as capital transfers from the rest of the UK (or, more precisely, affluent parts of England) to Wales. These are in the nature of free gifts, so create no accumulation of international indebtedness.

By contrast, if Wales were left to stand alone, its payments deficits (unsupported by free capital transfers) would quickly exhaust its holdings of gold and foreign exchange reserves. Thereafter, international trade would continue, but only to the extent which could be maintained on the basis of foreign exchange earned by Welsh exports. The Welsh economy would adjust, reaching a lower level of real income. At this level, the demand for imported goods would be compatible with the foreign demand for Welsh exports.

An independent nation can live beyond the means of its current earnings on the basis of its previously accumulated wealth assets, or upon the basis of gifts and loans received from the rest of the world. Wealth assets are finite. Loans must be repaid. Gifts are rarely forthcoming as a continuous arrangement. Unlike Wales, an independent nation cannot sustain in perpetuity an imbalance between earnings and expenditure.

If the balance of payments is ever a problem, it is the problem of having to face the necessity of adjusting to a lower standard of living, either because of macroeconomic policy having sought to attain a level of aggregate demand which the nation's resources cannot sustain, or because of changed circumstances having reduced the nation's capacity to achieve a given level of real income. In post-war Britain it resulted inevitably from the stop–go application of inflationary budgetary policy. Its 'success' during successive boom phases of the cycle was at the expense of an increasing volume of international debt.

Not surprisingly, having to face these realities was an unattractive proposition. The persistent recurrence of the 'balance of payments problem' in the UK has been accompanied by a number of alleged solutions which fall short of the necessity to reduce living standards. Whatever their damaging side effects, this is not to argue that exchange controls, import controls, devaluation, honours for export industry chairmen, and floating exchange rates do not have a role to play in obtaining a solution. It is the belief that these are *alternatives* to a lower living standard, rather than the *means* to achieve that necessary reduction, which is fallacious.

10 Macroeconomic Demand Management

> Full employment policies, as at present practised, attempt the quick and easy way of giving men employment where they happen to be, while the real problem is to bring about a distribution of labour which makes continuous high employment without artificial stimulus possible. (Hayek, 1967, p. 275)

KEYNES'S VIEW OF MERCANTILISM

According to Keynes, the mercantilist preoccupation with the trade balance was *not* (as Classical economics insisted) 'little better than nonsense'. Given that the rate of interest and the level of investment do *not* self-adjust to levels compatible with full employment, there was an 'element of scientific truth' in this disgraced doctrine.

An economy in Keynes's archetypal unemployment equilibrium faces two problems: it is short of remunerative investment opportunities at home and it requires the means to secure a reduction in the domestic rate of interest. Here, the mercantilist objective – a trade surplus – provided a remedy in three parts: overseas markets gave new outlets for domestic industries and so higher returns on investment; foreign currency offered the means to finance investment overseas or, alternatively, by adding to the domestic circulation, it would exert downward pressure upon interest rates.

It is generally apparent throughout *The General Theory* that Keynes was dealing with problems which are peculiar to the money economy. In an international context, variations to the money supply (and, according to Keynes's analysis, variations in the rate of interest) are largely dependent upon the balance of payments; from whence are derived the 'avowedly national advantages' of the mercantilist doctrine. Yet, because mercantilism was unashamedly a beggar-my-neighbour approach, it also gave a tendency to drift into war. Clearly, the doctrine was seriously flawed! According to Keynes, the mercantilists had 'perceived the existence of the problem without being able to push their analysis to the point of solving it' (Keynes, 1936, p. 350). The solution which they had missed was that of applying the policy of an autonomous rate of interest, unimpeded by international preoccupations, and of a national investment programme directed to an optimal level of domestic development. (ibid., p. 349)

In contrast to the mercantilist zero-sum game of trade balances, this option was open to all, so that all countries are able to achieve this end to reach the quite remarkable result of 'restoring economic health and strength internationally' (ibid.).

In its application during the post-war period, the achievement was short of the promised international concord. Problems were especially acute for the UK economy, with its heavy reliance upon overseas trade. A prerequisite of the Bretton Woods fixed exchange rate system was that trading partners should pursue budgetary policies of the same ilk. While this proved more or less the case during the initial years, differences in the degree to which Keynes's budgetary strategy was implemented were associated with differences in (ever-increasing) rates of inflation. For the UK, this experience was joined with that of intermittent sterling crises, as the Bank of England found it necessary to defend the fixed dollar parity each time it was threatened by a surfeit of sterling flowing from recurring trade deficits. The precise nature of these difficulties is described by the monetary theory of the balance of payments, which was summarised in Chapter 9.

LESSONS OF THE KEYNESIAN EXPERIMENT

The 1980s will be remembered as the decade in which the governments of western democracies decided that the balance of evidence was against Keynesianism; that attempts by fiscal measures to protect labour from changes demanded by the market process should be abandoned as damaging to productive efficiency and to economic prosperity.

Challenged not only by events, Keynesianism faced an intellectual assault in the revival of traditional (or Classical) economics. In this, Monetarism was central. The co-existence of high levels of unemployment and high rates of inflation was the common feature of the 1970s, and one which Monetarism was able to explain, convincingly, to a wide body of opinion. The Monetarist link between money and prices is an inherently plausible explanation for inflation. Make-work schemes of the type suggested by Keynes, when (for exaggerated effect) he advocated that the Treasury might

> fill old bottles with bank-notes, bury them at suitable depths in disused coal-mines ... and leave it to private enterprise on the well tried principle of *laissez-faire*, to dig the notes up again. (Ibid., p. 129)

were inherently implausible – at least as long-term solutions to the problem of unemployment.

In the original context of Keynes's advocacy of public sector deficits (that of chronic business recession), a reasoned case was made for real wages to be reduced by a modest but general increase in prices. Those who held to the forced saving doctrine warned that the provision of new bank credit would inevitably lead to price distortions and inflation. Although unreasonably dismissive of their logic, Keynes did acknowledge that, with the restoration of less extreme business conditions, the problem of persistent inflation would be faced.

In the aftermath of the Second World War, many western governments were intent that interest rates should remain low. By this, not only was it hoped to keep down the cost of servicing the National Debt (inflated by high wartime borrowing), it was also expected to encourage more rapid post-war reconstruction. The inevitable consequence was monetary expansion and ever escalating price inflation.

Further enticement had come from the initial belief that the Phillips curve promised a trade-off between inflation and unemployment; but during the 1960s doubts began to grow, as evidence accumulated to suggest that the trade-off was far from stable. For these new circumstances, the Friedman–Phelps job search analysis gave the 'expectations-augmented' Phillips curve, which explained why any short-term trade-off between unemployment and inflation could not last.

THE FORMATION OF EXPECTATIONS

According to Milton Friedman and Edmund Phelps (whose analyses were developed separately), job seekers (and hirers) accommodate expectations of future price increases (the result of expansionary demand management policies) into the wage bargain. However, the *manner* in which those expectations are formed was never adequately explained. Rather it was asserted that individuals would adapt slowly (rather than immediately) to actual events. Moreover, their ability to discover for themselves the events which preceded those price increases in a *causal sense*, were given no express consideration.

For example, even where the use of the printing press to finance profligate public expenditure programmes is generally recognised, the assumption of slowly 'adaptive expectations' insists that the effect which this has upon prices and wages *must first occur* before people even begin to adjust their expectations. This is implausible.

More recently, an alternative to the 'adaptive expectations' hypothesis has come to the fore, its path made easier by the trail blazed by Monetarism. This is the hypothesis of 'rational expectations', the brainchild of J.F. Muth in the early 1960s. Still more recently, it has taken the title of the New Classical School. Its distinctive attribute is that it does not set economic decision-takers apart by the extent of their assumed knowledge of how the economy behaves. More to the point, the government is declared to have no superior knowledge upon which to base its policy decisions. This is the hypothesis of rational expectations.

RATIONAL EXPECTATIONS

Economic decisions are those which necessarily entail an opportunity cost. In arriving at an economic decision, individuals are assumed to make best use of the information and resources at their disposal. Once acted upon, decisions will have an impact upon subsequent events; and so economic decisions require prior assessment of the future pattern of events both for the case where action is taken and for where it is not taken. In short, the formation of expectations about the future is a prerequisite for the judgement which has to be made.

Individuals are assumed to behave rationally; they are assumed to identify a desired outcome ('goal') and to behave in a manner which (given *their* understanding of the likely outcome of their action or inaction) moves them closer to that goal. Where such behaviour governs the acquisition and the assessment of information necessary for the formation of expectations about the future, individuals are said to form rational expectations.

How much time should be given to acquiring knowledge, the value of which cannot be assessed until it is known? In both this, and the decision which is taken upon the basis of that knowledge, it is inevitable that mistakes will be made. With hindsight some will have invested too few resources in the acquisition of information; some too many. On balance, across a large number of individuals, what is the likely distribution of mistakes? By the principle of insufficient reason, the supposition is that as many will get it wrong as get it right; that errors will be random rather than systematic. To this extent, by the postulate of rational expectations, individuals as a whole will acquire and use information efficiently.

What are the implications of rational expectations for changes in monetary policy? Such changes will have an immediate impact upon economic activity, with repercussions extending into a future of undefined length; but the *ultimate* impact of *monetary* disturbances upon *real* economic activity will be neutral. Monetary disturbances will have no lasting impact upon those real forces – guided by patterns of demand and supply – which determine the most efficient allocation of limited economic resources, because individuals will adjust fully to whatever new level of money aggregates are established.

Although Keynes's *General Theory* examined the short-term impact of policy changes upon macroeconomic aggregates, it did not pretend to argue that direct fiscal action was any more than an expedient measure to deal with an unusual set of historical conditions. While chapter 24 contains some whimsical proposals to change the features of capitalism, by allowing state investment to deprive 'capital of its scarcity value within one or two generations' (ibid., p. 377), the overriding objective was to explain the persistence of current unemployment and to suggest immediate remedies; but while Keynes began with the realistic assumption that unemployed resources were available for immediate use, this same assumption destroys the need to apply economic principles. Hayek's perceptive criticism remains widely neglected:

> An analysis on the assumption of full employment, even if the assumption is only partially valid, at least helps us to understand the functioning of the price mechanism, the significance of the relations between different prices and of the factors which lead to changes in these relations. But the assumption that all goods and factors are available in excess makes the whole price system redundant, undermined and unintelligible. (Hayek, 1972, p. 103)

Price signals allow individuals to access whichever particular set of information is necessary for them to arrive at efficient cost-effective decisions. It is by the exercise of independent initiatives in the pursuit of self-advancement that the economy advances; and it is this same exercise of initiative in the formation of rational expectations which would deny the government any purposeful macroeconomic demand management role.

THE DISAPPEARING PHILLIPS CURVE

The earliest macroeconomic application of the hypothesis of rational expectations, was an investigation of the short-run trade-off between unemployment and inflation across different countries (Lucas, 1973). The statistics indicated that the Phillips curve relationship existed only when macroeconomic policy had made no attempt to use it! Where monetary policy *had* been used to finance fiscal deficits (with the intention of boosting employment), higher levels of inflation were not associated with lower rates of unemployment. The inflation/unemployment trade-off existed only when there had been no attempt to manipulate it for political ends.

In this particular example is illustrated the most profound implication for macroeconomic demand management. It is that to be able to direct the economy – to produce an outcome which is broadly predictable – requires that there exist well-defined relationships between economic variables which themselves will be *unaffected* by the implementation of any particular set of policies. In short, unless there are immutable laws of macroeconomics, attempts to manipulate the system may be frustrated by changes in the relationships. Just as the Phillips curve relationship disappears if attempts are made to use it as a fulcrum for policy, there is evidence (see Neftci and Thomas, 1978) that changes in (macroeconomic) patterns of behaviour coincide with changes in the regime of monetary policy.

Aside from the statistical evidence, the assumption of non-rational expectations must be untenable if specialist advice can be traded profitably. Here, an efficient market would always drive decisions towards those which are rationally based; and by this same argument, the government could never expect to outmanoeuvre the general public upon the basis of its own expertise.

CROWDING OUT

The implications of this conclusion may be understood by its association with the hypothesis of 'crowding out'. This is the argument that attempts to expand aggregate demand by increasing public expenditure will necessarily be offset by reductions in private components of aggregate demand. For example, where financed by borrowing from the banking sector, the money supply will increase, and prices will rise to reduce the real purchasing power of private incomes; where financed by borrowing from the non-bank private sector, interest rates will rise to deter private investment expenditure and (by its inducement to higher saving) to reduce private consumption expenditure; where financed by taxation of incomes, consumers' expenditure will fall (or alternatively saving will fall, to cause interest rates to rise).

Consider further the example of profligate public expenditure, and suppose that it is financed this time by borrowing from overseas. Neither domestic prices, nor interest rates, nor current taxation need be affected. So surely there would be no crowding out? Not according to the New Classical School. With rational expectations, individuals form the widest view of the consequences of public expenditure policy. The loan *will* require eventual repayment, so *will* require monetary expansion, higher interest rates or higher taxation at some future date. Private expenditure plans will be tailored to meet those expectations.

Even if the loan from abroad were to be presented as a gift, the situation would be only slightly changed. Enhanced purchasing power (by the value of the gift) would be largely deferred to the future in order to avoid the repercussions of sharp readjustments to expenditure patterns. The present impact of such a gift would be minimised by individuals forming rational expectations of the consequences, not only of their own actions, but (more importantly) those of policy-makers.

It is because individuals will have a view of the appropriate balance between their own expenditure and savings out of current earnings that they will react. So, to the extent that personal incomes *might* have been temporarily raised by fiscal expansion, saving would have increased in order to meet those rationally expected tax demands (or to offset reduced real income either from price inflation, or from higher interest rates) in the future.

Crowding out is an idea which can stand alone, separate and

distinct from rational expectations; but the former can be deduced from the latter. Under the rational expectations hypothesis, public sector expenditure will *always* crowd out private expenditure; so there can be no basis for macroeconomic demand management to be effective in securing either a better present or a better future.

Effective demand management relies upon the inability of individual economic decision-takers to acquire *any* insight into how the economy works. Under such conditions, individuals would be unable to react (or, at least, be very slow to react) to the effects of fiscal expansion. Increases in prices, interest rates or taxation would not cause reductions in private expenditure *pro rata* with the increase in public expenditure; and only under those circumstances would crowding out not occur.

THE NEW CLASSICAL SCHOOL

In refusing to acknowledge that the government holds, in any sense, a superior position, the New Classical School took an opposite extreme. Price distortions were fully anticipated because it was assumed that individuals never made mistakes of interpretation. The full implications of a policy change were understood, anticipated and counteracting behaviour precisely attuned to offset any impact which the policy change might have had upon real economic magnitudes. Output and unemployment remained unchanged.

Thus, Muth's original analysis (Muth, 1961) implied that individuals were fully informed of the 'true' processes at work; that they were able instantaneously to gauge the effects of policy changes upon their own position, and to adjust their own behaviour without expectation of error. Though this case is pedagogically instructive, it is neither realistic nor is it rational in the usual economic sense of that adjective. Rational behaviour is that which derives from utility maximisation.

Subsequent to Muth's pioneering work, the New Classical School has tended to define rational expectations in this latter sense. Individuals are assumed to apply reason to knowledge of their circumstances, but the implausible presumption that those circumstances are perfectly known is avoided. Rather, all that is required is that systematic behaviour should involve the more frequent repetition of successful strategies and the shifting away from unsuccessful ones. Inevitably this must lead to a distribution of individuals' expectations around the rational outcome. Keynes held to a similar position in 1930:

> action based on inaccurate anticipations will not long survive experiences of a contrary character, so that facts will soon override anticipation except where they agree. (Keynes, 1930, p. 160)

Without the assumption of immediate and instantaneous adjustment, attention must be given to the time-path of the equilibrating process. Time is required for individuals to gauge the ever changing structure of the economy together with all the nuances of economic policy adjustments. Two further complications may also be suggested: currently formed rational expectations rely upon estimates of the future, while the future must be affected by decisions based upon those rational expectations (see Shiller, 1978, p. 38). Moreover, the suggestion that the authorities might anticipate rational expectations and formulate policy to keep one step ahead of consequential changes in behaviour (see Maddock and Carter, 1982, p. 48) arbitrarily stops at this second stage of strategical planning. Convolutions such as these can give rise to any number of theoretical possibilities.

With obfuscation of this kind, Keynesians keep alive the potential for fiscal intervention; for, despite the evidence, there is still a reluctance to abandon the notion of some trade-off between unemployment and inflation. One argument is that a controlled measure of price inflation loosens those wage and price rigidities which hinder adjustment within a dynamic labour market. Another, that the interests of social cohesion are served by a more equitable distribution of the costs of economic change. Whatever the strength of these arguments, they must be weighed against the unwelcome effects of monetary expansion; that is, the distortions to the structure of production which cannot be sustained.

Not only was that generation of economists, which had been nurtured on Keynes's *General Theory*, impressed by the historical evidence of Phillips curves, it also suited the authorities to believe that they might disregard the monetary impact of fiscal deficits to engineer a trade-off between a tolerable rate of inflation and jobs. Although the institution of collective bargaining became a scapegoat for the creeping inflation which, under those influences, soon began to stride out, the short-term electoral popularity drawn from monetary laxity constitutes more than circumstantial evidence of governmental culpability.

It is ironic that the comparative static methodology of *The General Theory*, so much criticised by Robertson and Hayek, should have been discarded by economists seeking to defend the Keynesian revolution during its twentieth-century demise. Great emphasis is now given to the view that quantity adjustments might outpace price adjustments to leave the economy at rest with less than full employment; that dynamic considerations establish the case for intervention by the authorities for the common good. The irony is the greater in that the original theoretical developments within the New Classical School adopted the comparative static framework to analyse the implications of adjustments under the assumption of rational expectations.

In some ways ideas have come full circle; but Keynesianism will remain unassailable to eyes that wish to to see it so:

> a government sensing that its Keynesian policies are taking it out of its depth may rather than plunging on anyway, flounder back to the shallow end ... the same episode which, to some, appears as 'almost drowning' would appear to those with a disposition, no matter what, to keep their aspirations up, as 'almost swimming'. (Coddington, 1983, pp. 121–2).

11 Inflation

> If Keynes were alive, the theory might have been extended and strengthened, but that work has not been carried out by his successors. As a result, Keynesianism today – in practice, as an influence on policy – is inflationary in effect, and consistently inflationary. (Rees-Mogg, 1974, p. 27)

MONEY AND INFLATION

Inflation is a continuous rise in the price of goods and services in terms of the nominal money unit. Inflation cannot occur in a barter economy: it is purely a monetary phenomenon – a conclusion which monetary authorities may attempt to deny, when they fail in their responsibility to maintain a sound currency. Labour unions are the most common scapegoat; but in addition to cost-push by unions, inflation has been blamed upon sharp increases in the price of primary products, and upon cartel-inspired increases in the cost of oil. Yet, if labour-based, raw materials-based or energy-based commodity prices all rise continuously, it is more likely that they are the symptoms of a common cause.

Wage setting by monopoly labour unions may raise the relative cost of more labour-intensive commodities; but this is not a cause of inflation. Rather it is a direct cause of unemployment; and if unions retard the pace of adjustment to changes in market conditions that, too, is a direct cause of unemployment. Where wages are kept above market rates, labour is in excess supply. Similar considerations would give rise to a surfeit of raw materials and of oil where those prices are kept artificially above the market rate. It is the failure to allow adjustment to be directed by the market process, not the new conditions themselves, which inevitably leads to the underutilisation of resources of whatever kind; and monetary expansion cannot help to achieve that adjustment. Rather, it confuses price signals, disrupts the market process, and sets in train the process of inflation, while leaving original problems unresolved.

Cost-push theses of inflation deny the primacy of money. They are associated with Keynes because of the emphasis which he gave to the inflexible structure of wage relativities. Cost-push theses may also be traced to Keynes's assertion that, under full employment, long run price stability would

> depend on the strength of the upward trend of the wage-unit (or, more precisely, of the cost-unit) compared with the rate of increase in the efficiency of the productive system. (Keynes, 1936, p. 309)

Cost-push theses reached their zenith in the 1970s (see, for example Wiles, 1973; Hicks, 1975; and Kahn, 1976), since when their common philosophy has been outmoded by events. As government has withdrawn support from industries in decline, and has refused any responsibility for setting criteria for annual wage awards, relativities have been shaken down, and market realities are now more readily acknowledged. The weight of evidence has brought a general rejection of cost-push theses and a return to the view that excessive monetary expansion is *the* cause of inflation, although it will always remain possible for academic wizardry to conjure an esoteric scenario to demonstrate otherwise (see, for example, Hahn, 1982).

THE STAGES OF INFLATION

Notwithstanding the inflationary tendencies unleashed by Keynes-inspired budgetary strategies of western democracies, the experience of inflation predates Keynes and has a history as long as that of state involvement with the provision of currency. Monetary mismanagement allows for a ready addition to tax revenues; and the need to finance large state expenditures has been a common origin of price inflation throughout history.

The Austrian economist Ludwig von Mises has categorised the typical course of inflation into three stages (Rothbard, 1976, p. 175). The first stage is associated with the extraordinary expenses of war. These are universally regarded as temporary, so that the rise in prices, which is expected to occur as a consequence, is also expected to be only temporary. At this stage, the demand for money rises, because the public expects the purchasing power of money eventually to appreciate when prices revert to normal levels. The effect of this enhanced demand for money is to limit the rise in prices to a rate which is below that of the increase in the money supply.

The successful acquisition of funds by the authorities – at zero interest cost and without the expected inflationary impulse –

encourages further monetary expansion but, as prices continue to rise, the public's expectations begin to change. The erosion of purchasing power is increasingly felt, and is no longer regarded as likely to be reversed, so that money balances are reduced as portfolio assets are adjusted to an optimum mix. The greater the rate of inflation, the lower the proportion of assets held as money. Prices now begin to rise faster than the rate of monetary expansion, and a second stage begins.

The German inflation of 1921–23 provides the classic example (see Rees-Mogg, 1974, p. 36). The war years had brought an increase in the money supply of 340 per cent, accompanied by a 139 per cent increase in prices. Between November 1918 and July 1919 there was a further 57 per cent increase in money when, again, prices rose to a lesser degree. Prices began to gain ground during the next six months, rising by 185 per cent compared with a 33 per cent increase in the money supply. Thereafter, inflation moved rapidly into its second phase as, from May 1921 to July 1922, money rose by 149 per cent and prices by 635 per cent.

With prices rising faster than the money supply, there is the beginning of a money shortage. Individuals strive to bring income receipts into ever closer proximity with expenditure and so, while the demand to hold money (in its dimension of duration) remains low, in terms of volume it increases (because of the ever rising money values of transactions). Illustration again comes from the German inflation, when employees were allowed time off work at ever shorter intervals, in order to spend their earnings. At the same time, the Reichsbank found that printing notes in ever greater denomination was the most effective way to bring the required amount into circulation to meet the ever escalating transactions demand.

The third and final runaway stage of inflation brings the collapse of the currency and a flight from money into anything; when any purchase is preferable to the retention of money. The damage done to the allocative efficiency of the price mechanism during the first and second stages is as nothing to this final collapse of money and breakdown of the economic order.

MONEY AND KEYNES'S *GENERAL THEORY*

Employment, interest and money, rather than money and inflation, were given emphasis in *The General Theory*. According to Keynes, money created distinct differences from a barter economy. It generated unique forces. Money was the financial bridge between the time when an investment decision is taken and the moment of its full gestation. Keynes's failure to deal explicitly with the question of finance for investment was clarified by later comments. Neither the instantaneous multiplier nor the balanced budget multiplier were of any practical significance. Money is the key. Funds liquidated by the culmination of earlier projects serve to finance later projects, but *higher* levels of expenditure require *additional* money (see Fletcher, 1987, p. 113).

Here the banking system and, in particular, the practice of allowing overdraft facilities was important. The assertion was that, in a non-barter economy, new money finance is required to mobilise unemployed resources. New money is necessary to finance new investment expenditure which is accommodated by real resources freed by *additional* saving only as the latter is forthcoming from *additional* income. There was no need for prior saving, nor was there any recognition of the role of forced saving.

Acceptance of these arguments swept aside the problem of resource allocation to allow an uninhibited push for increased production and employment. *The General Theory* discounted the inflationary significance of the initial impact of monetary expansion upon prices. Instead, stress was placed upon the immediate stimulus to output and employment arising from the prices-induced reduction in the level of real wages.

Later still came the convenient thought that doubt might be cast upon the inverse relationship between real wages and unemployment. Where there was spare capacity, statistical time series for labour productivity appeared to contradict the expectation of diminishing returns to labour, so that labour might benefit from increased employment with no diminution of real earnings. Keynes was even to suggest that statisticians would be employed to guide policy-makers by identifying the exact point where marginal costs start to rise as capacity constraints are met (see Keynes, 1939, p. 45).

This afterthought fixed firmly in mind, Keynesians could assert: 'The classical theory of the real wage is really an irrelevant element of the *General Theory* and ought to be discarded' (Thirlwall, 1981, p. 24). With this reckless abandon there was created a curious economy, a world of no trade-offs, and its features were not lost upon politicians of the centre-left. The implications were astounding, for now trade lost as a result of high unit costs could be regained by deficit-financed government expenditure. Unemployment was no longer to be explained by the failure of price adjustment within labour markets. Deficient demand was the cause and relative wage adjustment an irrelevancy.

WAGES AND PRICES AT FULL EMPLOYMENT

The continuous and rapid readjustment of relative wages is desirable at all times and is paramount under conditions of full employment. Of this there is virtually nothing within *The General Theory*. There, longer term considerations are concerned with levels of wages and prices set in the context of high aggregate demand sustained by public investment programmes. Various bottlenecks would emerge such that involuntary unemployment would be removed in some sectors of the economy before others, so that the first signs of *true* inflation – Keynes's term for the situation where money wages would rise *pro rata* with the increase in prices – would begin to appear before the final eradication of involuntary unemployment.

Yet, even before true inflation is experienced, rising prices could have undesirable effects upon the real economy, setting in trend developments which could not be sustained. For example, rising unit costs might be underestimated so that entrepreneurs are misled by rising sales proceeds into overexpansion (see Keynes, 1936, p. 290); but Keynes gave no particular emphasis to distortions such as this. Quite the opposite; for in a bold statement comes the breathtaking assertion that

> whilst a deflation of effective demand below the level required for full employment will diminish employment as well as prices, an inflation of it above this level will merely affect prices. (Ibid., p. 292)

In the first instance, the provision of new money to finance the expenditure necessary to raise effective demand can drive real sectors of the economy to otherwise unattainable heights; but at the ultimate, it will *merely* affect prices. So it remained only to pick the optimal point along the spectrum of real expansion/true inflation trade-off; an idea which was to underpin the short-lived notion of a stable Phillips curve relationship between inflation and the rate of unemployment. Were it so simple!

If bottlenecks can occur *before* involuntary unemployment is eliminated, then why not *after* its elimination? Then, if the effects of monetary expansion were not uniform, some prices would rise faster than others and price relativities would be disturbed, with consequences for the real economy. It is implicit that Keynes took the effects upon prices to be non-uniform before full employment (with bottlenecks causing early price increases in some parts of the economy) but uniform beyond that point, for otherwise their impact would not be *merely* to affect prices. Keynes nowhere explains the asymmetry.

This neglect extended to the labour market, where transactions were set against the background of a fixed industrial structure. The UK had been slow to respond to advancing technology and greater competition during the early inter-war years and, in the many sectors which were in natural decline, unemployment was inevitable. Yet, the need for differential readjustments was ignored and great emphasis given to general aspects of the malaise; and so Keynes considered it 'reasonable' that workers should resist reductions in money wages which were not of an 'all-round character'. Deficient demand was the problem, for which only public expenditure financed by monetary expansion could provide the solution.

The assumption was that relative prices and relative wages might be taken *as given*; but it was an assumption which destroyed the very nature of the economic problem, namely the efficient allocation of scarce resources within an economy in which technology and tastes are continually changing. The alleged solution was to inaugurate an inflationary process where the effects upon price relativities were assumed not to exist. A theory of employment constructed upon this assumption provided no useful blueprint for economic policy, and so this must constitute a fundamental flaw in Keynes's *General Theory*.

Still now, recognition of the impact of inflation upon price relativities is lacking, not only on the part of the public and policymakers, but even among professional economists. Although inflation is widely recognised to be one of the major economic problems, there is scant understanding of the nature of the disruption it brings – a reflection of the degree to which the work of both Hayek and Robertson has been neglected both during and since the era of *The General Theory*.

The General Theory held that an increase in the general level of prices must be understood upon the same basis as an individual price increase; that is, as 'governed by the conditions of supply and demand' (Keynes, 1936, p. 292). Many factors lay behind the rise in unit costs as output is raised. These included the skill quality of the labour employed, the productivity of equipment, bottlenecks in production, increases in the 'wage unit' and rising raw materials costs; but the most important of these – changes in the wage unit – did not 'readily lend themselves to theoretical generalisations' (ibid., p. 302) for they depended upon many factors, including the psychology of workers, and the policies pursued by employers and trade unions.

Here and elsewhere is recognition of the unsolved problem of true inflation; and it was echoed in later years

> Of course, I do not want to see money wages forever soaring upwards to a level to which real wages cannot follow. It is one of the chief tasks ahead of our statesmanship to find a way to prevent this. (Keynes, 1944, p. 430)

In this Keynes was aware of the importance of historical forces. Price stability during the nineteenth century was

> due to a balance of forces in an age when individual groups of employers were strong enough to prevent the wage unit from rising much faster than the efficiency of production, and when monetary systems were ... sufficiently fluid and sufficiently conservative ... [to give] ... the lowest rate of interest readily acceptable by wealth owners. (Keynes, 1936, p. 308)

The advent of modern communications, cheaper transport and greater competition, brought benefits to working men, which emergent labour unions were quick to claim as their own achievements. These, together with the later commitment to social welfare programmes and high aggregate demand, reduced the threat of unemployment which is a natural feature of the market process. In its assumed absence, which was the promise of Keynes's recommendations for the conduct of economic policy, there is no evidence that Keynes gave any consideration to the kind of institutional mechanism which might offset the upward pressure on wages. This was a curious omission given the recognition that 'there is naturally for all groups a pressure in this direction, which entrepreneurs will be more ready to meet when they are doing better business' (ibid., p. 301).

Keynes argued that any policy to control inflation had to be concerned with those factors which determined the various supply responses to changes in demand; but while he was later to recommend the use of buffer stocks to bring greater stability to primary commodities' prices, no suggestions were ever forthcoming with respect to rising wage costs. Rather, it was left for followers to voice vague aspirations that productivity gains from higher growth would ameliorate the problem. In particular, the influence of Nicholas Kaldor during the Chancellorship of James Callaghan was responsible for a Selective Employment Tax in 1966, which was imposed upon the allegedly low productivity growth service sectors. The idea was to shift the workforce towards the favoured manufacturing sectors in order to raise the general rate of productivity growth. Both theoretically and practically the notion was a failure and, certainly, it made no contribution to the rising problem of inflation.

INCOMES POLICY

Although Keynes made no recommendation that the state might adopt the kind of detailed control of prices and incomes which was attempted in many western nations during the high inflation decades of the 1960s and 1970s, administrative structures for the determination of wages – that is, incomes policy – are within the spirit of Keynes's faith in a rational approach to national economic management.

Incomes policy was a logical development of cost-push theories of inflation, which were born out of Keynes's analysis of the origins of an increase in the general level of prices. The post-war evolution of incomes policy may be traced to Lord Beveridge's acclaimed *Full Employment in a Free Society*, published in 1944, in which he coined the phrase 'vicious wage-price spiral' which was to epitomise cost-push theses; but his warnings of the inflationary consequences of sustained high demand brought only a weak policy counterpart in exhortations, and vague guidelines for private sector settlements.

Survey work (Lester, 1946; Wilson and Andrews, 1951) had suggested that prices were set on a cost-plus basis without regard for the optimal conditions as determined by marginal analysis. Wages simultaneously determined both costs of production (and hence prices) and consumers' income; so with the reputation of the Quantity Theory of money in tatters, the blame for inflation could only be directed at those responsible for setting wages.

Appeals for 'reasonable behaviour' in wage bargaining were to become the prelude to more formal constraints imposed intermittently over the next quarter-century: but sweetness and light were no more to be expected from labour unions than from hard-nosed company negotiators. Even had this been so, by what mechanism would cost-push theorists have explained how new money generated by fiscal deficits might be absorbed into circulation without creating a general upward pressure upon prices (including the price of labour)? Where fiscal deficits persisted, it was common to find incomes policy in association with prices policy. Although ceilings upon price levels mitigated labour unrest, inflation continued in its 'repressed' form, which is the worst kind, for it 'makes the price mechanism wholly inoperative and leads to its progressive replacement by the central direction of all economic activity' (Hayek, 1972, p. 115).

Incomes policy was an inevitable consequence of the full employment strategy and it threatened the efficient interchange of information which is signalled only by changes in relative wages and prices. Fortunately, the damage to the free market process was gradual and the brink was approached at a pace which allowed time for the lessons of experience to have their accumulating effect. When the corollary of fiscal deficits was shown to be monetary expansion and creeping inflation, policy moved on to more formal constraints upon both public and private sectors. While disciples of Keynes discussed alternative proposals for incomes policy with enthusiasm, the doubters, many of whom had warned of the inflationary consequences of deficit finance, only reluctantly accepted its role to act as a brake upon rapidly soaring inflationary expectations (see Shenoy, 1972, pp. 4–6).

INDEXATION AND WAGE BARGAINING

Friedman and Hayek have expressed opposite views of the effect of price indexation as an instrument for reducing the trauma of adjustment from high inflation. Friedman believes that it is possible to bring about a more rapid end to inflation by adopting measures which reduce the distortions arising from unanticipated inflation/deflation. Where the usual practice is for wage bargaining to set nominal rates, unanticipated inflation/deflation alters the real terms of the settlement. The introduction of escalator clauses into agreements allows each side to give full attention to the reality of conditions within their own market-place.

Friedman's case is that escalators can have no direct impact upon the rate of inflation. Rather, they simply ensure the avoidance of the price distortion caused by inflation. Friedman concedes the possibility that, by making it more easy for the public to recognise changes in the rate of inflation, adjustment lags would be reduced 'and thus make the nominal price level more sensitive and variable' (Friedman, 1974, p. 31), but he suggests the existence of a beneficial trade-off in that more sensitive nominal prices imply less sensitive and, therefore, more stable real values. Indexation would have the effect of stabilising the real terms upon which wage and price contracts are first agreed. Friedman sees this as ameliorating the effects of inflation, and as a first step towards its elimination.

A similar consideration is to be found in *The General Theory*, but with a different conclusion:

> If, indeed, some attempt were made to stabilise real wages by fixing wages in terms of wage goods, the effect could only be to cause a violent oscillation of money-prices. For every small adjustment in the propensity to consume and the inducement to invest would cause money prices to rush violently between zero and infinity. (Keynes, 1936, p. 239)

Here, Keynes recognises the role of price relativities – rare indeed in *The General Theory*! Fluctuations in the aggregate demand for consumers' goods must be accommodated (with given nominal wages) by adjustment of the nominal price level of 'wage goods', for any attempt to stabilise the purchasing power of income would cause the prices of 'wage goods' to fluctuate wildly.

Friedman and Keynes are referring to aggregate price and wage levels, and each of their conclusions is correct in its own context; Friedman's that of inflation, Keynes's that of real adjustment in a non-inflation world. The problem comes in telling the situations apart. When is a price increase not representative of general inflation? Answer: when it is a real adjustment to changed demand/supply conditions.

The difficulty is that adjustments to real prices and wages are required continuously both under inflation and non-inflation; and these adjustments need not necessarily have a neutral impact upon whichever index of prices is adopted to trigger escalator clauses. In other words, Friedman implicitly makes the assumption that it is possible to conjure an index of inflation which is unaffected by price increases of a non-monetary origin, but there are many circumstances where this would be difficult. To illustrate, conflict in the Middle East, and a rise in the level of energy prices, would have a large impact upon an index of prices which, if it caused automatic increases in wages, would lead to widespread unemployment.

Hayek's view of the value of price indices is no different from his view of 'the fashionable pseudo-scientific economics of averages' (Hayek, 1972, p. 20). The fact that price averages move differently in different countries is no proof of a tendency of the price structure of a country to move as a whole. Certainly, there is no means of deciding, because of a movement in the price average, that a particular money wage for a particular job or a particular price for a particular contract is no longer appropriate.

Such thoughts lead Hayek not simply to reject the usefulness of indexation but to indicate a number of dangers. Indexation would make inflation more tolerable in the short term and so reduce resistance to it. In wage bargaining, indexation would strengthen the claim for money wage increases in line with inflation, of those whose real wages (because of changed market circumstances) ought to fall. Not least, indexation would mean that changes to the structure of real wage relativities could be achieved only by increases of all except the lowest nominal wages, so making continuous inflation necessary. In short, indexation is 'bound in the long run to make the whole wage structure more and more rigid and thereby lead to the destruction of the market economy' (Hayek, 1978, p. 79).

12 Free Markets, Monetarism and the Austrian School

[T]hings are too fluid, too complex, too mutually involved, too elusive, subjective, subtle, too much subject to learning processes, too evolutionary, restless and fertile of surprise to yield a scheme of ascertainable, reliable and permanent parameter estimates. (Shackle, 1969, p. 292)

THE LEGACY OF KEYNES

Industrialisation required change in the organisational structure of commerce. During the eighteenth and nineteenth centuries this had been continuously forced by the market process. There were adjustments to new specialisations and to growing economic interdependence. Rapid growth brought material advancement and proved capable of supporting an ever larger population, although hardship was experienced during intermittent periods of trade recession.

Man's abilities to harness nature's energies, to adapt himself quickly from peacetime to wage large-scale wars, and then to revert to peaceful coexistence, was a striking, if not wholly beneficial, feature. Yet, the contrast between the productive efficiency of wartime economies, and the wasteful unemployment experienced during times of peace was unsettling.

While human ingenuity seemed capable of finding rational solutions to technological problems, the promotion of employment, economic growth, sound currencies, and international trading arrangements satisfactory to all, appeared as elusive goals. Problems of this kind attracted attention which became focused in 'technocracy', a belief set in rationality that – free from political value judgements – science could provide solutions to social problems; only the right expertise was required. This was the approach taken by Keynes in formulating a conceptual framework for problems which he considered to be inherent in a capitalist monetary economy.

Keynes voiced two concerns. One was the need for immediate

action to give work to the unemployed. In times of peace, government expenditure programmes might be equally as effective in placing men in work as mobilisation for war. The difference – the implications of which Keynesian economics has never acknowledged – is that the consensus for the production of guns and tanks during war is unlikely to be repeated with respect to peacetime production. Even at war, and with the coexistence of a just cause, inspired leadership, and powerful allies, the co-ordination of production and shipment is an unwieldy business. At peace, with no common view of the composition of government-financed output, there exists not even the crudest of guides to direct production. Certainly, the level of economic welfare to be gained by a rational approach is unlikely to approach that obtained from allowing free rein to the market process.

Keynes's second concern covered this objection. It was that market forces could not be relied upon to sustain a high employment level of output. That being so, there would be no allocative welfare loss from government expenditure for, in its absence, those resources would remain permanently unemployed. Keynes believed that the economy could be manipulated while still allowing for the market system to achieve allocative efficiency;

> When 9,000,000 men are employed out of 10,000,000 willing and able to work, there is no evidence that the labour of these 9,000,000 men is misdirected. The complaint against the present system is not that these 9,000,000 men ought to be employed on different tasks but that tasks should be available for the remaining 1,000,000 men. (Keynes, 1936, p. 379)

It was simply a question of finding something for the 1 000 000 to do; but there would be no repercussions for the 9 000 000. In this Keynes failed to anticipate the political pressures to protect industries in decay which, with the involvement of government, were to become symptomatic of the malaise arising from full employment policies in post-war Britain.

Keynes was impatient with the pace of economic recovery. His new analysis showed that delay would result from a rate of interest kept unduly high by liquidity preference; and also by the low rate of return on capital. More generally, the market could produce perverse reactions. The collapse of the New York Stock Exchange had clouded Keynes's view of the nature of financial markets. The more organised financial markets became, the more likely they were to be dominated by short-term speculation as dealings in securities became further removed from 'either active or prospective' knowledge of 'the business in question'. In effect, Keynes was a critic of the efficient market theory before ever that term was coined;

> We are assuming, in effect, that the existing market valuation, however arrived at, is uniquely *correct* in relation to our existing knowledge of the facts which will influence the yield on investment, and that it will only change in proportion to changes in this knowledge; though, philosophically speaking, it cannot be uniquely correct, since our existing knowledge does not provide a sufficient basis for a calculated mathematical expectation. (Ibid., p. 152)

From a detailed examination of this fundamental objection, Keynes concluded that private entrepreneurship offered no means to secure a full employment level of investment; and so he advocated 'a somewhat comprehensive socialisation of investment' (ibid., p. 378). Unlike private entrepreneurship, continuously diverted by its preoccupation with short-term gains, the state was in a unique position 'to calculate the marginal efficiency of capital-goods on long views and on the basis of general social advantage' (ibid., p. 164). Why this was the case and how it was supposed to happen were not explained. Questions of definition and determination of the national interest, or 'general social advantage', were not raised.

MACROECONOMIC THEORIES

The greater is the use of money in the organisation of human affairs, the greater is the degree of uncertainty; for the very existence of money implies uncertainty on the part of its users. Expectations are formed; but no general propositions can be established to indicate reactions when expectations turn out to be wrong. Having identified the particular nature of the problem, Keynes intended that his *General Theory* would point to a solution; but there could be no general solution for there are no fundamental laws relating to time series of statistical averages of economic data. While these may prove the basis for retrospective appraisal of historical events, broad aggregates can convey little, if any, information necessary to make macroeconomic forecasts of the future. Whatever particular success macroeconomic theories and their statistical models might have, they run inevitably into historical and institutional obsolescence: 'It is the shifting, inconstant, and unstable nature of expectations which makes "a general macroeconomic theory" an impossible misnomer' (Hutchinson, 1980, p. 17).

With no general features upon which to rest the centrally important role of expectations, Keynes's arguments, of necessity, were based upon the more readily apparent socio-economic patterns of the time. For example, the proposition that real wages could be reduced by a deliberately engineered rise in commodity prices must have seemed reasonable, given that money wages had failed to adjust fully to the experience of unprecedented price deflation.

Although Keynes prescribed state intervention to achieve close control of the level of aggregate demand, widespread state ownership of the means of production formed no part of *The General Theory*. From this, many left-of-centre democrats believe that Keynes gave governments the opportunity to ensure the survival of capitalism, by removing its less attractive features. Yet, in choosing to adopt the scientific approach of modern economics, Keynes relinquished any philosophical appeal to priorities between objectives. If, by inference, the approach is recognised now as a matter of prudence – of giving priority to the problem of unemployment – this was a political, not an economic decision. Indeed, this much is to be drawn from the 'Concluding Notes' of *The General Theory*, where there is an expressed fear of authoritative state systems. Problems associated with 'capitalistic individualism' had to be tackled: there had to be a more equal distribution of income and a wider opportunity of employment, the absence of which were the 'outstanding faults' of contemporary society.

Keynes believed that aggregate demand management would avoid the inefficiencies of command economies; but because expenditure and fiscal policies were never intended to be neutral, it was inevitable that they became associated with resentment, with jealousies and with a more widespread interventionism of a highly specific nature. For even as Keynes's ideas were beginning to take hold, capitalism was bringing the erstwhile luxury of mobility and communications to the working class; and enhanced competition within local labour markets began to remove the yawning disparities in the standard of living of employees and employers.

Keynes and his generation had lived their formative years in advance of this transformation, when élitist paternalism was regarded as enlightened behaviour. Perhaps its last vestige was heard with

Lord Stockton's *cri de coeur*, likening the privatisation of state assets to the sale of the family's silver.[1]

The idea of policy-making in the hands of charitable politicians and a disinterested body of expert bureaucrats is flawed. If it ever had its moment, it belonged to the colonial era; for whenever economic decisions were removed from the market-place in twentieth-century Britain, rationality became subjugated by political clout. Even if it were once expedient, Keynes's remedy for widespread unemployment was to prove poison in these new circumstances. Not just the economic context, but also the political and social structure which prompted *The General Theory* did not last.

MONETARISM AND THE AUSTRIAN SCHOOL

Keynesianism is defunct. In its place is Monetarism, a modern version of the Quantity Theory which 'constitutes the most serious qualification to the thesis of the limitations of general macroeconomic theories' (Hutchinson, 1980, p. 18). Its objective, as a theory of the demand to hold money, is much less ambitious than Keynes's theory of output and employment. Monetarism *per se* contributes nothing towards a rational approach to aggregate demand management. For this reason, it is closely aligned with the Austrian School which sets itself against such an approach. Even so, the concentration upon broad money aggregates, measures of income and wealth, and the artefacts of price and wage indices, which is the hallmark of Monetarism, is an anathema to the Austrian School. Even this more limited approach to macroeconomics is regarded as pseudoscientific. This is the crucial philosophical difference between the modern champions of the Austrian School and of the Quantity Theory, respectively Hayek and Friedman.

The original antecedents of the Austrian School may be traced from Carl Menger to Ludwig von Mises, a contemporary of Keynes, who argued specific points of dissension with the traditional Quantity Theory. With money as the unit of account, the price of all other commodities can be expressed in money terms; and the purchasing power of money may be expressed as the inverse of the price level of each and every commodity which is traded for money. This vast array of commodities is heterogenous, so it is impossible to establish a single unitary price level figure for money. Any attempt to capture this concept within an average index number (in order to measure changes in the purchasing power of money) conjures up a totality of goods whose *relative* prices are assumed to remain unaltered. In principle, this assumption can find no home within the Austrian paradigm, where price relativities *necessarily* are changed by the process of monetary expansion.

The importance of relative prices to the market process, and the disturbances caused by monetary fluctuations, are at the heart of the Austrian criticism of the Quantity Theory and, it must be said, Monetarism; but animosity is not unbridled. Each camp rises unashamedly in the defence of free enterprise, capitalism and individual freedom, all of which were threatened by the quest for 'technocracy' in economics. Furthermore, as Monetarists have become more interested by refinements to the rational expectations hypothesis, so the Viennese and the Chicago traditions have found more common ground.

CHANGE, INCENTIVES AND THE MARKET PROCESS

The idea that public expenditure and fiscal aggregates might be manipulated to bring a prosperity which evades the market process has no empirical and little theoretical support. Furthermore, the commitment to full employment undermined the discipline of market forces, with the effect of slowing the pace of technological change and economic advance. This was inevitable, given the objective of Keynesian analysis, which takes full employment and not efficient production as its goal. Socialist republics demonstrate that full employment is not difficult to achieve, providing there is no requirement to provide the goods and services which people (but not *the* people) want.

The attempt to maintain output and employment regardless of performance removes incentives and the stimulus to change. As damaging in its impact upon the market process was the effect of policy upon money and prices, for the *interdependence* of monetary and fiscal policy implies that fiscal deficits necessarily involve government borrowing, usually obtained from a compliant banking system, which produces monetary growth and inflation.

The market operates by price signals, feeding information to producers and consumers, and without which balance between supply and demand is unattainable. By distorting those price signals, inflation disrupts the market process with the consequence of unwanted surpluses of some commodities and shortages of others. Far from achieving positive results, macroeconomic demand management introduced inefficiencies and distortions which have left the economy materially worse off.

Macroeconomics came close to providing the intellectual justification for a corporate tyranny. Whether arrived at from capitalism, through the intermediate stage of the mixed economy, or more directly through national socialism, the centralised direction of consumption, savings and investment decisions destroys individual liberty in its pursuit of an asserted national interest. When governments assume responsibility, it is inevitable that business, organised labour and the public at large will come to rely upon the guarantee of no failure, which is a sure path to mediocrity.

In addition, the distortions are manifest on a different plane, for self-interest is as much the prime mover of political parties, government departments and agencies as it is of private business. In consequence, the direction of policy will tend to favour producer-interest groups rather than consumers. This happens because most voters earn their living from one activity while their expenditure is spread across a wide range. Producer-interest is more likely to be cost-effective in influencing government than that of consumers, who have no organisational base to compare with that of trade unions and employers' groupings. Furthermore, where there is a common interest, government departments and agencies may combine with producer groups to exert concerted pressure upon government policy.

The physical sciences have long abandoned the idea of perpetual motion. For fifty years the science of economics was mesmerised by the promise of a similar impossibility. This is that planned intervention by government can maintain national output at levels which cannot be sustained by the free market; that government intervention can achieve use of land, labour and capital for which entrepreneurial activity can devise no useful schemes. What was on offer was *not* a compassionate framework for social policy, but the suggestion that a greater *economic* benefit could somehow be achieved. In this, there was no substance: 'the popular success of socialist arguments forged by trained economists is not due to their scientific merits but to the fact that they fall in with the cravings of the human heart' (Schumpeter, 1954, p. 281). Where realisation has been achieved, the lesson has been learned the hard way; from experience rather than from thought. The return to the private sector of large areas formerly taken into state control offers considerable gains. In this the electorate has understood more than politicians of the left, and even the majority of the academic economics profession. It is not so much that economists have too long imbibed Keynesian macroeconomics, but rather that the profession has attracted to it those with a leaning to that particular brand of socialist intervention. The message is surely now clear to those who wish to see. The 'comprehensive socialisation of investment' offers no economic returns. It is not simply that the government is impotent, but that its intervention in the economy is so often an impediment to economic efficiency.

Although a role remains for government, it is modest and relates exclusively to *micro*economics. Without some degree of intervention there can be little doubt that colluding business and powerful groups of organised labour contrive to fetter the free market in order to further narrow sectional interests. So it is necessary for the government to establish a legal framework to preclude such behaviour. In addition, a legislative role may be necessary to compensate for obvious instances of market failure, although these will be limited in extent. Too easily market failure can be replaced by government failure. The government has also a duty to administer its welfare system and to raise its tax revenue in a manner which maintains the incentive to work. This much is required in order to gain economic efficiency at its highest level. More than that ensures that it can never be attained.

13 Postscript: When Keynes was a Monetarist

> Keynes's *Tract on Monetary Reform* (1923) was largely forgotten as the economics profession swung toward the Keynes of the *General Theory*. (Dorn, 1987, p. 13)

It is significant that during the post *General Theory* period Keynes did not repudiate his early writings on money. Although, even before it went to press, Keynes recognised *A Treatise on Money* as the premature and confused expression of revolutionary new ideas, his earlier work – *A Tract on Monetary Reform* – is a masterpiece without blemish. It deserves greater attention. Indeed, Friedman has expressed the opinion that the *Tract* is 'the most explicitly monetarist work amongst the writings of the Cambridge School' (Presley, 1985, p. 2).[1] The reasons derive from the book's principal concern which is that savings, investment, production, and employment depend upon stability in the value of money; that, without a scientific understanding of money matters, the order of society is threatened.

Value will continue to be assigned to ideas within *The General Theory*, but not to the detriment of fundamental insights derived from three centuries of refinement to the Quantity Theory of Money. These include Keynes's asset demand for money and the earlier important contribution of the *Tract*, where, as always, Keynes's observations were guided by contemporary history. The arguments which follow are reported from this neglected precursor of Monetarist analysis.

INFLATION AND BUSINESS ACTIVITY

Business prosperity in the nineteenth century had been soundly based upon the savings of the whole community. This had been made possible by constancy in the value of money; but there was no guarantee. The message of history was that no prolonged war, nor any social upheaval, had ever occurred without progressive currency depreciation. Where this was on a large scale, attitudes towards saving and investment were affected. This was no accident, for currency depreciation is the result of two driving forces; the 'impecuniosity of governments and the superior political influence of the debtor class' (Keynes, 1923, p. 9). There is one solution; that is, for it to become the primary objective of state policy to maintain a stable standard of value.

The *Tract* identifies a more insidious evil arising from the stimulus to business from persistent inflation. Business becomes all too easy. Stock appreciation provides an effortless addition to profits, and leads habitually to commodity speculation. Slow adjustment of the money rate of interest to rising prices forces down the real rate, even to a negative value. This brings further windfall profits, and the cumulative effect is that businessmen lose their conservative instincts, thinking more of potential speculative gains than the future of their business.

To the ordinary man, inflated profits are viewed as the *cause* of inflation and there is a natural resentment. By turning businessmen into profiteers, inflation threatens capitalism itself. It acts to discourage investment and to discredit enterprise. Purported remedies themselves undermine the market: that is, subsidies, price and rent fixing, and so on. In due course comes reaction and depression, when large losses replace windfall gains. In these changed circumstances, business holds as little stock as possible, with the effect of bringing industries into decline.

Violent change to the standard of value adds confusion to those real factors which determine the distribution of income and wealth. The distinction between capital and income becomes lost, and accumulated savings may be unwarily dissipated in consumption expenditure.

A change in the value of money would be of no consequence if it affected all transactions equally; but this does not happen. Inflation redistributes income in a fashion which injures savers and benefits business. Those who are able correctly to anticipate its effects can gain at the expense of others. On the whole, it may benefit earners; but its most striking consequence is its injustice to those who have committed their wealth to titles in money rather than to things. Deflation works in the opposite direction, by overburdening business to the advantage of the rentier class; but depression has a further penalty which it imposes as much in the form of unemployment as by lowering real income.

Whereas movements in *relative* prices are an important instrument to secure the correct proportions of goods under current production, this is patently untrue of movements in the *general* level of prices. When prices are *expected* to fall, production is inhibited. When prices are *expected* to rise, output expands. Yet, variations in the value of money affect neither the needs nor the productive capacity of the economy, nor the desired amounts of goods to be produced. In recognition of this, Keynes recommends counteractive monetary policy which, even if only partially successful, would constitute an improvement on the policy of allowing inflation to take its course.

INFLATION AND PUBLIC FINANCE

The *Tract* highlights the implications of inflation for public finance. Governments obtain resources as readily by printing money as by levying taxes; but special advantages are attached to the former because the public finds its effects especially hard to evade. Inflation taxes all those who hold currency notes. The burden of the inflation tax is well spread, it is difficult to evade, it costs little to collect and it falls roughly in proportion to the wealth of the victim. The only recourse for the public is to alter its habits in the use of money, but this, as experience shows, is slow to occur.

Lessons drawn from inflation in Austria, Germany and Russia were lost to the perpetrators of 'Keynesianism' in the post-1945 period:

> It is common to speak as though, when a Government pays its way by inflation, the people of the country avoid taxation. We have seen that this is not so. What is raised by printing notes is just as much taken from the public as is beer-duty or an income tax. What a government spends the public pay for. (Ibid., p. 62)

Nevertheless, Keynes shows that money will continue to be used even with high rates of inflation since, for example, if

> the rate of inflation is such that the value of money falls by half every year, and ... that the cash used by the public ... is turned over 100 times a year ... then this is equivalent to a turnover tax of 1/2 per cent on each transaction. The public would gladly pay such a tax rather than suffer the trouble and inconvenience of barter (Ibid., p. 49)

The full impact of considerations of this kind were to be developed within the Monetarist framework (see Friedman, 1969).

Inflation raises revenue for governments; but it has a second function. It erodes the burden of the National Debt. In many cases, the size of the latter may demand special attention, but there are other solutions. The National Debt can be reduced to manageable proportions either by repudiation or by a deliberate tax on wealth, with the latter option affording the greater degree of social cohesion.

THE COURSE OF INFLATION

In tracing the sequential course of a currency inflation, Keynes produces an argument distinctly Austrian in character.[2] At first, there is faith in money as the ultimate standard. When prices begin to rise, the public defers purchases believing that it can wait for prices to fall. A larger amount of money is held than before. Eventually, a second stage sets in. Recognition of the true impact of inflation leads the public to economise in its holdings of money. Expenditures are brought forward. Use may even be made of foreign money. The attempt to minimise money balances implies that recourse to borrowing may prove necessary. The public then faces high rates of interest, increasing towards and often beyond the anticipated rate of depreciation of money.

In the last stages of inflation, a soaring velocity of circulation has a greater effect in raising prices than monetary expansion itself. A point is reached where the public cannot further economise on its use of money; so that even the slightest moderation in its mistrust of the future value of the currency leads to an increase in the amount of money balances held. By this stage, the gold value of domestic currency is at a very low figure, so that the government, if it has any resources at all, finds itself able to maintain the exchange rate. The value of the currency bottoms out.

INFLATION AND MONETARY POLICY

Keynes stresses the central importance of the Quantity Theory. When individuals have more cash than they require for transactions purposes, they get rid of the surplus by buying goods or investments. Their demand to hold money depends upon their required purchasing power, which in turn depends partly upon wealth and partly upon habits in the use of money. All things considered, there is a direct relationship between the quantity of money and the level of prices. While in the long term a doubling of money causes prices to double, in the short term, money is not an independent variable in the Quantity Theory equation. To concentrate only upon long term relationships is improper:

> In the long run we are all dead. Economists set themselves too easy, too useless a task if in tempestuous seasons they can only tell us that when the storm is long past the ocean is flat again. (Ibid., p. 80)

Changes in the quantity of money will change habits, through the impact upon income distribution and patterns of money hoarding, upon expectations, and upon the distribution of wealth. All such factors affect the amount of cash (in proportion to transactions) which individuals choose to hold, the proportion of their liquid assets deposited with banks, and banks' own liquid assets ratios.

Again, an active monetary policy is advocated. The primary tool is that of the Bank Rate, although there is doubt that it affords sufficient power. To achieve price stability, the authorities must be prepared to vary both the money supply and the banks' required ratio of liquid assets. The duty of the authorities must be to keep each of these under close control; to use these levers to counter changes both in the public's use of money and the banks' own dealings.

INTERNATIONAL TRADE, EXCHANGE RATES AND CURRENCY MARKETS

From a discussion of the purchasing power parity theory of exchange rates, Keynes reflects upon the implications for governments using monetary expansion to cover budget deficits. He objects to a common view that exchange rate stability is achieved through sound budgetary and Bank Rate policies. While international payments must be continuously in balance, trade flows never are. Seasonal trade imbalances must be counter-balanced by money flows and these will exert pressure upon exchange rates.

Without fixed exchange rates, bankers have no certainty that the arbitrage profit will be sufficient to offset the risk of accommodating trade imbalances. Unforeseen exchange rate movements can bring heavy losses. Where trade imbalances are large, the exchange rate must rise/fall until either the speculative financier moves in, or the trader becomes so appalled by the exchange rate offered that he forgoes his trading deal.

Keynes was strongly of the opinion that speculative currency deals should not be discouraged. Regulations are never watertight, and are a source of excessive profits to middlemen. More importantly, speculators provide an essential service. By discouraging professional currency speculation, the authorities cause such services to command a premium; an unnecessary handicap to trade.

The forward exchange market may be used by traders to cover against exchange rate uncertainty. The difference between the spot and the forward price of currency rests upon a number of determinants; short-term interest rates; the threat of financial trouble or political disturbance; the relative demand/supply of currencies; and the degree of competition in the respective markets. There is no theoretical reason why there should not be an excellent forward market in a highly unstable currency; a market which might usefully be supported by central banks. With free access to forward markets, no trader need run an exchange risk unless he wishes to. With all these, the *Tract* offers modern insights into a market which in the 1920s was in its early stages of development.

Keynes questions the objective of restoring sterling to the gold standard, whether achieved through deflation or devaluation. Deflation is harmful to business and it threatens social cohesion. It throws extra burdens upon taxpayers by increasing the value of the National Debt. Devaluation harms those who acquire fixed interest stock at the exchange rate prior to monetary expansion. Without doubt this is unjust; but the greater proportion of such stock may have been obtained after inflation was under way. True justice requires differential valuation adjustments, which is hardly practical. Deflation and devaluation both cause injustices; but devaluation does less harm.

FIXED EXCHANGE RATES VERSUS PRICE STABILITY

Is it more important that a currency should retain constant purchasing power, or that there should be constancy in its value against other currencies? According to the *Tract*, fixed exchange rates are not a panacea, and may even weaken monetary control. A stable exchange rate cannot be achieved without stability of both internal and external prices; and the latter lie outside the domestic authority's control. The right choice is not the same for all countries. It depends upon the importance of foreign trade; but there is a presumption in favour of stable prices. Exchange rate stability is a convenience which adds to the profitabilty of foreign trade. Price stability avoids the greater evils associated with inflation and deflation. Nevertheless the reluctance to abandon gold is understandable; for 'a chief object of stabilising exchanges is to strap down Ministers of Finance!' (ibid., p. 169).

Monetary control requires a sound scheme to regulate the supply of currency and credit; and to regulate the supply of foreign exchange against the effects of seasonal trade. The credit creation capacity of commercial banks is determined by their total cash holdings, together with deposits held at the Bank of England. What determines the volume of cash? The single most significant factor is the excess of government expenditure over the amount secured from the public by taxation and borrowing. Thus, the capacity for credit creation 'is mainly governed by the policies and actions of the Bank of England and the Treasury' (ibid., p. 182).

Policy might be guided by reference to an index of prices, without judgement or discretion (as advocated by Irving Fisher, and forerunner of the Monetarist Rule); but to wait until a price movement is under way before taking action is undesirable. Rather, the authorities might promote a standard composite commodity as an objective standard of value:

> it would promote confidence and furnish an objective standard of value, if, an official index number having been compiled of such a character as to register the price of a standard composite commodity, the authorities were to adopt this composite commodity as their standard of value in the sense that they would employ all their resources to prevent a movement of its price. (Ibid., p. 187)

A radical idea in 1923, it is discussed but still regarded as such today (see Friedman, 1986, p. 65).

Keynes hints at discretionary measures of a kind which became the hallmark of post-1945 attempts to manage the economy; further research would reveal the criteria, other than the trend of prices, to guide monetary action by the authorities:

the state of employment, the volume of production, the effective demand for credit ... the rate of interest ... the volume of new issues, the flow of cash into circulation, the statistics of foreign trade and the levels of the exchanges must all be taken into account. (Ibid., p. 188)

In 1923, however, the *one* objective was stability of prices; and had this been achieved in the 1920s and 1930s, there would have been no need for the fiscal imagery evoked by *The General Theory*.

Appendix

The 'fiscal stance' is described by the difference between government expenditure (G) and tax revenue (T), which gives the public sector borrowing requirement ($PSBR$):

$$G - T = PSBR \tag{A1}$$

Fiscal expansion causes a rise in the $PSBR$ which must be met from one or more of three sources:

— additional borrowing from the banks (ΔGBB)
— additional borrowing from the non-bank private sector (ΔGBP)
— the issue of new notes and coins (ΔC)

(The latter is actually a subcategory, and could be included within the first two; for whether held by banks (ΔBC) or by non-banks (ΔPC), new cash holdings constitute additional interest-free loans to the government.) However, we now have

$$PSBR = \Delta GBB + \Delta GBP + \Delta BC + \Delta PC \tag{A2}$$

which is rearranged as

$$\Delta BC + \Delta PC = PSBR - \Delta GBB - \Delta GBP \tag{A3}$$

A change in the money supply (ΔM) is defined to be the sum of new cash in circulation (ΔPC) plus any net increase in bank deposits (ΔBD). By accountancy conventions, the latter (the net increase in bank liabilities) is necessarily equal to the net increase in bank assets; that is, additional cash held by banks (ΔBC) plus any net increase in loans extended to the general puplic (ΔPBB) and to the government (ΔGBB). Thus, by definition

$$\Delta M = \Delta PC + \Delta BC + \Delta PBB + \Delta GBB \tag{A4}$$

rearranging,

$$\Delta BC + \Delta PC = \Delta M - \Delta PBB - \Delta GBB \tag{A5}$$

Appendix

Then, taking together equations (A3) and (A5) gives

$$\Delta M - \Delta PBB - \Delta GBB = PSBR - \Delta GBB - \Delta GBP \qquad (A6)$$

so that

$$\Delta M = PSBR - \Delta GBP + \Delta PBB \qquad (A7)$$

This equation shows that the increase in the money supply (ΔM) comprises the *PSBR*, *less* that part of the latter which is met by the net increase in government borrowing from the non-bank private sector (ΔGBP), *plus* the net increase in bank lending to the private sector (ΔPBB).

Notes

2 Money

1. See Chapter 8
2. In the UK, the immediate impact of monetary deflation and the rapid rise in the cost of bank credit (supply side effects) in 1980–81 was to increase the demand for money (by individuals and firms which found themselves overcommitted in the changed circumstances). As the short-term demand for bank credit rose to abnormal heights, the commercial banks acquiesced and permitted 'distress borrowing'. For a period, both the demand to hold money and the supply of money increased, despite the deflationary impact of the deliberate reduction in the growth of high-powered money. This effect was enhanced by the inclusion of interest-bearing components in the definition of the aggregate money supply which caused the demand for money to grow more rapidly, as a response to higher rates of interest, until it reached a new equilibrium level (Laidler, 1986, p. 36). The upshot of the readjustments which took place was that supply side measures, directed by monetary policy, necessitated demand side accommodation which gave higher interest rates and a lower rate of inflation.

3 The Quantity Theory of Money

1. John Locke (1692) *Some Considerations of the Consequences of the Lowering of Interest and Raising the Value of Money*; David Hume (1752) 'On Money', in *Political Discourses*. See Kahn, 1984.
2. John Stuart Mill (1848) *Principles of Political Economy*. See Kahn, 1984, p. 39. [M], [V], etc. have been added.
3. Two Austrian economists had raised similar objections somewhat earlier than Marshall: Carl Menger (1892) *Geld* and Ludwig von Mises (1912) *The Theory of Money and Credit*. See Gilbert, 1953, p. 145.
4. Pigou here used a wider aggregate than real income; that is, 'total resources enjoyed by the community'. Wealth assets retained from earlier periods were thereby included with current output (Q) to jointly determine the demand to hold money. Although this increases the differentiation between the Yale and Cambridge versions, subsequent debate made more of their similarities than differences. See Kahn, 1984, p. 45.
5. Separate arguments here concern the expectations set in train by the *rate* at which prices are affected (either by monetary expansion or contraction), so that the price level may rise or fall more than proportionately with changes in the nominal quantity of money (see Gilbert, 1953, p. 155 ff). The features of a typical inflation are discussed in Chapter 11.
6. Knut Wicksell (1906) *Lectures on Political Economy*; Henry Thornton (1802) *An Inquiry into the Nature of the Paper Credit of Great Britain*. See O'Driscoll, 1977, p. 44.
7. 'The "natural rate of unemployment", a term I introduced to parallel Knut

Wicksell's "natural rate of interest", is not a numerical constant but depends on "real" as opposed to monetary factors' (Friedman, 1977, p. 15). Although it is true that the term 'natural rate' was coined by Wicksell, its conceptual base had been sketched by Ricardo and also by Thornton and Mill (see Patinkin, 1965, p. 367).

8. 'The rate of interest at which *the demand for loan capital and the supply of savings* exactly agree, and which more or less corresponds to the expected yield on the newly created capital, will then be the normal or natural real rate' (Knut Wicksell, *Lectures on Political Economy*, first published in Swedish in 1906. Cited from Gilbert, 1956, p. 69 fn).

9. Mr Winston Churchill was the Chancellor of the Exchequer who had responsibility for that policy.

4 Money, Relative Prices and the Rate of Interest

1. Most recently, however, Hayek has argued for an alternative framework for monetary control. See 'Hayek and the rejection of monetary policy' in Chapter 8.
2. Among the qualifications which have been raised is one by A.H. Hansen. It is the possibility that monetary expansion (lowering the market rate of interest) might redistribute income so as to produce an equal reduction in the natural rate of interest. Thus, however unlikely, it is theoretically possible for monetary expansion to be compatible with both price stability and equality between the market rate and the natural rate of interest (see Gilbert, 1956, pp. 75–6).
3. Most notable of the results were *Money* published in 1922, and *Banking Policy and the Price Level* published in 1926.
4. Richard Cantillon *An Essay on the Nature of Credit*. See Hayek, 1935, p. 9.
5. Although Keynes was to make this same point (Keynes, 1936, p. 83), he refused to accept the notion of forced saving. This is discussed in Chapter 6.

5 Keynes's *General Theory*

1. Whereas the transactions demand for money is stated in nominal terms, depending both upon the level of real income and upon prevailing prices, the speculative demand is for real balances. Keynes's assumption (for deep recession) of a constant price level permits the summation of M_1 and M_2.
2. While writers before Keynes had floated ideas closely aligned with Keynes's Liquidity Preference theory, few had attached any great importance to hoarding as a particular cause of unemployment (see Schumpeter, 1954, p. 1080).
3. See Chapter 4.

6 Forced Saving versus the Multiplier

1. This much can be agreed with an author who seeks to defend Keynes against his critics:

Without the establishment of a sequence in which causation flowed from investment to saving there could be no meaning to the principle of effective demand and no possibility of under-employment as an equilibrium state. (Fletcher, 1987, p. 68)

2. Over a long period, substantial changes in the rate of interest might tend to modify social habits and, thereby, affect the propensity to spend 'though in which direction it would be hard to say' (Keynes, 1936, p. 93). With regard to saving, the influence of changes in the rate of interest would be *in the opposite direction* to that usually supposed (see Keynes, 1936, p. 110); a low interest rate would stimulate investment, and raise both income and saving.
3. Keynes also acknowledges that writers of earlier centuries regarded 'insufficiency of the propensity to consume' as relevant to the evils of unemployment (see Keynes, 1936, p. 358).
4. Keynes did not approve of this comparison, preferring the description 'short period equilibrium' to 'instantaneous snapshot' (Fletcher, 1987, p. 88).
5. See Chapter 5.

7 Monetarism

1. Although the amount of human capital is not readily varied, its relative proportion may be varied by changing the amounts of other assets held in the portfolio.
2. This point is also made, in an aside, in *The General Theory* (Keynes, 1936, p. 84).

8 Control of the Money Supply

1. This was Tooke's *History of Prices and the State of Circulation*. See Congdon, 1981, p. 4.
2. Also, see Kaldor and Trevithick, 1981; and Kaldor, 1982.

12 Free Markets, Monetarism and the Austrian School

1. Lord Stockton's speech to the Tory Reform Group was reported in *The Times*, 9 November 1985.

13 Postscript: When Keynes was a Monetarist

1. Reported from a private letter.
2. See Chapter 11, where similar stages of inflation are reported from von Mises's *Theory of Money and Credit*, which was first published in German in 1912. As Keynes reviewed Mises's book in the *Economic Journal* of 1914, his failure to acknowledge this source is surprising. Perhaps it is to be explained by the comment that 'in German I can only clearly understand what I already know!' (Keynes 1930, p. 199n). The transition between the different stages of inflation is examined more fully by Friedman (1969, pp. 12–13).

References

M.J. ARTIS, and D.A. CURRIE (1981) 'Monetary Targets and the Exchange Rate: A Case for Conditional Targets', in W.A. Eltis and P.J.N. Sinclair (eds), *The Money Supply and the Exchange Rate* (Oxford: Clarendon Press) pp. 176–200.

N.P. BARRY (1978) 'Austrian Economists on Money and Society', *National Westminster Bank Quarterly Review*, (May) 20–31.

M. BLAUG (1978) *Economic Theory in Retrospect*, 3rd ed. (Cambridge: Cambridge University Press).

R. BOOTLE (1984) 'Origins of the Monetarist Fallacy – the Legacy of Gold', *Lloyds Bank Review*, vol. 153 (July) 16–37.

C.E. CHALLIS (1978) *The Tudor Coinage* (Manchester: Manchester University Press).

V. CHICK (1986) 'Keynes' *General Theory* After Fifty Years: What Remains?' University College London Discussion Paper No. 86–18.

C. CLARK (1970) *Taxmanship*, 2nd ed. (London: Institute of Economic Affairs).

G. CLAYTON, J.C. GILBERT and R. SEDGWICK (1971) *Monetary Theory and Policy in the 1970s* (London: Oxford University Press).

A. CODDINGTON (1981) *Keynesian Economics: The Search for First Principles* (London: George Allen & Unwin).

T. CONGDON (1978) *Monetarism; An Essay in Definition* (London: Centre for Policy Studies).

T. CONGDON (1980) 'The Monetary Base Debate: Another Instalment in the Currency School vs Banking School Controversy?' *National Westminster Bank Quarterly Review* (August) 2–13.

T. CONGDON (1981) 'Is the Provision of a Sound Currency a Necessary Function of the State?', *National Westminster Bank Quarterly Review* (August) 2–21.

J.A. DORN (1987) 'The Search for Stable Money: An Historical Perspective', in J.A. Dorn and A.J. Schwartz (eds) *The Search for Stable Money: Essays on Monetary Reform* (Chicago and London: University of Chicago Press) pp. 1–28.

R. DORNBUSCH (1976) 'Expectations and Exchange Rate Dynamics', *Journal of Political Economy*, vol. 84, no. 6 (December) 1161–77.

J. FENDER (1981) *Understanding Keynes* (Brighton: Wheatsheaf Books).

I. FISHER (1911) *The Purchasing Power of Money* (New York: Macmillan).

G.A. FLETCHER (1987) *The Keynesian Revolution and its Critics* (London: Macmillan).

M. FRIEDMAN (1956) 'The Quantity Theory of Money: a Restatement', in M. Friedman, *Studies in the Quantity Theory of Money* (Chicago: University of Chicago Press) pp. 3–21.

M. FRIEDMAN (1959) 'Statement on Monetary Theory and Policy', in *Employment Growth and Price Levels* (Hearings before the Joint Economic Committee, 80th Congress 1st session, 25–28 May) (Washington DC: U.S. Government Printing Office) pp. 605–12.

References

M. FRIEDMAN (1968) 'The Role of Monetary Policy', *American Economic Review*, LVII, no. 1 (March) 1–17.
M. FRIEDMAN (1969) 'Post-war Trends in Monetary Theory and Policy', in M. Friedman *The Optimum Quantity of Money and Other Essays* (London: Macmillan) pp. 69–79.
M. FRIEDMAN (1970) *The Counter-revolution in Monetary Theory* (London: Institute of Economic Affairs).
M. FRIEDMAN (1974) *Monetary Correction* (London: Institute of Economic Affairs).
M. FRIEDMAN (1977) *Inflation and Unemployment: The New Dimension of Politics* (London: Institute of Economic Affairs).
M. FRIEDMAN (1986) 'Quantity Theory of Money (Survey Article for New Palgrave Dictionary of Political Economy)', Working Papers in Economics No. E-86-7 (The Hoover Institution, Stanford University, February).
M. FRIEDMAN (1987) 'Monetary Policy: Tactics versus Strategy', in J.A. Dorn and A.J. Schwartz (eds) *The Search for Stable Money* (Chicago and London: The University of Chicago Press).
J.K. GALBRAITH (1961) *The Great Crash* (Oxford: Clarendon Press).
J.C. GILBERT (1953) 'The Demand for Money: The Development of an Economic Concept', *Journal of Political Economy* (April) 144–59.
J.C. GILBERT (1956) 'Changes in Productivity and the Price Level in a Closed Economy', *Yorkshire Bulletin of Economic and Social Research*, vol. 8, no. 2 (November) 61–79.
J.C. GILBERT (1959) 'Economic Theory and Policy', *Yorkshire Bulletin of Economic and Social Research*, vol. 11, no. 1 (July) 1–18.
J.C. GILBERT (1982) *Keynes's Impact on Monetary Economics* (London: Butterworths).
C.A.E. GOODHART (1984) *Monetary Theory and Practice* (London: Macmillan).
J.D. GOULD (1970) *The Great Debasement. Currency and the Economy in Mid-Tudor England* (Oxford: Clarendon Press).
F.H. HAHN (1982) *Money and Inflation* (Oxford: Blackwell).
F.A. HAYEK (1933) *Monetary Theory and the Trade Cycle* (London: Jonathan Cape).
F.A. HAYEK (1935) *Prices and Production*, revised ed. (London: Routledge & Kegan Paul).
F.A. HAYEK (1939) 'A Note on the Development of the Doctrine of "Forced Saving"', *The Quarterly Journal of Economics*, vol. XLVII (November, 1932), cited from *Profits, Interest and Investment and Other Essays on the Theory of Industrial Fluctuations* (London: Routledge & Kegan Paul) pp. 183–97.
F.A. HAYEK (1942) 'The Ricardo Effect', *Economica*, vol. IX (New Series) no. 34 (May) 127–52, reprinted in *Individuals and Economic Order* (London: Routledge & Kegan Paul) pp. 220–54.
F.A. HAYEK (1943) 'A Commodity Reserve Currency', *Economic Journal*, vol. 53 (June/September) 176–84.
F.A. HAYEK (1960) *The Constitution of Liberty* (London and Henley: Routledge & Kegan Paul).

F.A. HAYEK (1967) *Studies in Philosophy, Politics and Economics* (London: Routledge & Kegan Paul).
F.A. HAYEK (1972) *A Tiger by the Tail* (London: Institute of Economic Affairs).
F.A. HAYEK (1973) 'The Place of Menger's *Grundsatze* in the History of Economic Thought', in J.R. Hicks and W.Weber (eds) *Carl Menger and the Austrian School of Economics* (Oxford: Clarendon Press) pp. 1–14.
F.A. HAYEK (1975) *Full Employment at Any Price?* (London: Institute of Economic Affairs).
F.A. HAYEK (1978) *Denationalisation of Money – The Argument Refined*, 2nd ed., Hobart Paper 70 (London: Institute of Economic Affairs).
J.R. HICKS (1946) *Value and Capital*, 2nd ed. (Oxford: Clarendon Press).
J.R. HICKS (1975) 'What is Wrong with Monetarism?', *Lloyds Bank Review*, vol. 118 (October) 1–13.
T.W. HUTCHINSON (1980) *The Limitations of General Theories in Macroeconomics* (Washington, DC: American Enterprise Institute).
E.S. JOHNSON and H.G. JOHNSON (1978) *The Shadow of Keynes* (Oxford: Blackwell).
H.G. JOHNSON (1975) 'Keynes and British Economists', in M. Keynes (ed.), *Essays on John Maynard Keynes* (Cambridge: Cambridge University Press) pp. 108–22.
R.F. KAHN (1976) 'Thoughts on the Behaviour of Wages and Monetarism', *Lloyds Bank Review*, vol. 119 (January) 1–11.
R.F. KAHN (1984) *The Making of Keynes' General Theory* (Cambridge: Cambridge University Press).
N. KALDOR (1960) 'Professor Hayek and the Concertina Effect', *Economica* vol. IX (New Series) no. 35 (November, 1942) 359–82, reprinted in Kaldor, *Essays on Economic Stability and Growth* (Illinois: Glenco) pp. 148–76.
N. KALDOR and J.A. TREVITHICK (1981) 'A Keynesian Perspective on Money', *Lloyds Bank Review*, 139 (January 1981) 1–19.
N. KALDOR (1982) *The Scourge of Monetarism* (London: Allen & Unwin).
J.M. KEYNES (1923) *A Tract on Monetary Reform* (London: Macmillan).
J.M. KEYNES (1930) *A Treatise on Money* (London: Macmillan).
J.M. KEYNES (1936) *The General Theory of Employment, Interest and Money* (London: Macmillan).
J.M. KEYNES (1937) 'The General Theory of Employment', *Quarterly Journal of Economics*, vol. LI (February) 209–23.
J.M. KEYNES (1939) 'Relative Movements of Real Wages and Output', *Economic Journal*, vol. 49, (March) 34–51.
J.M. KEYNES (1943) 'The Objective of International Price Stability', *Economic Journal*, vol. 53 (June/September) 185–7.
J.M. KEYNES (1944) 'A Rejoinder to Professor Graham', *Economic Journal*, vol. LIV (December) 429–30.
A. KLAMER (1984) *The New Classical Macroeconomics* (Brighton: Wheatsheaf Books).
J.A. KREGEL (1979) 'A Keynesian Approach to Inflation Theory and Policy', in D. Heathfield (ed.) *Perspectives on Inflation* (London: Longman) pp. 189–216.

D. LAIDLER (1986) 'Monetary Policy in Britain: Successes and Shortcomings', *Oxford Review of Economic Policy*, vol. 1, no. 1, 35–45.
A. LERNER (1944) *The Economics of Control* (New York: Macmillan).
R.A. LESTER (1946) 'Shortcomings of Marginal Analysis for Wage Employment Problems', *American Economic Review*, vol. 36, no. 1 (March) 63–82.
R.E. LUCAS (1973) 'Some International Evidence on Output-Inflation Trade-offs', *American Economic Review*, vol. 63, no. 3 (June) 326–34.
R. MADDOCK and M. CARTER (1982) 'A Child's Guide to Rational Expectations', *Journal of Economic Literature*, vol. XX (March 1982) 39–51.
R.C.O. MATTHEWS (1968) 'Why Has Britain Had Full Employment since the War?', *Economic Journal*, vol. 78, no. 3 (September) 555–69.
F. MODIGLIANI (1950) 'Liquidity Preference and the Theory of Interest and Money', *Econometrica*, vol. 12 (1944) 45–88; cited from American Economic Association, *Readings in Monetary Theory* (London: George Allen & Unwin) pp. 186–239.
N. MONSARRAT (1943) *East Coast Corvette* (London: Cassell).
L.S. MOSS (1976) 'The Monetary Economics of Ludwig von Mises', in L.S. Moss, *The Economics of Ludvig von Mises* (Kansas City: Sheed & Ward) pp. 13–49.
L.S. MOSS and K.I. VAUGHN (1986) 'Hayek's Ricardo effect: A Second Look', *History of Political Economy*, vol. 18, no.4, 545–65.
J. MUTH (1961) 'Rational Expectations and the Theory of Price Movements', *Econometrica*, vol. 29, no. 3 (July) 315–35.
S. NEFTCI and S. THOMAS (1978) 'A Little Bit of Evidence on the Natural Rate Hypothesis from the US', *Journal of Monetary Economics*, vol. 4, no. 1 315–19.
J.P. O'DRISCOLL, Jr (1977) *Economics as a Co-ordination Problem* (Kansas City: Sheed, Andrews & McMeel).
D. PATINKIN (1965) *Money, Interest and Prices*, 2nd ed. (New York: Harper & Row).
E.S. PHELPS (1968) 'Money Wage Dynamics and Labour Market Equilibrium', *Journal of Political Economy*, vol. 76, 678–711.
A.W. PHILLIPS (1958) 'The relationship between unemployment and the rate of change of money wage rates in the United Kingdom, 1861–1957', *Economica*, vol. 25, 283–99.
J.R. PRESLEY (1979) *Robertsonian Economics* (London: Macmillan).
J.R. PRESLEY (1985) 'Modern Monetarist Ideas: A British Connection?', Research Paper No. 13 (Loughborough University Banking Centre).
W. REES-MOGG (1974) *The Reigning Error: The Crisis of World Inflation* (London: Hamish Hamilton).
Report of the Committee on the Working of the Monetary System (1959) Cmd 827.
D.H. ROBERTSON (1966) 'A Survey of Modern Monetary Controversy', in *Essays in Money and Interest* (selected with a Memoir by Sir John Hicks) (Glasgow: Collins) pp. 105–37.
D.H. ROBERTSON (1966) 'Mr Keynes and the Rate of Interest', in *Essays in Money and Interest* (selected with a Memoir by Sir John Hicks) (Glasgow: Collins) pp. 105–37.

A. ROBINSON (1947) 'John Maynard Keynes, 1883–1946', *Economic Journal*, vol. LVII (March) 1–68.
M.R. ROTHBARD (1976) 'The Austrian Theory of Money', in E.G. Dolan (ed.), *The Foundations of Austrian Economics* (Kansas City: Sheed, Andrews & McMeel).
J. RUEFF (1964) *The Age of Inflation* (Chicago: Gateway Editions, Henry Regnery).
J.A. SCHUMPETER (1954) *History of Economic Analysis* (London: Allen & Unwin).
G.L.S. SHACKLE (1967) *The Years of High Theory* (Cambridge: Cambridge University Press).
G.L.S. SHACKLE (1969) *Decision, Order and Time in Human Affairs* (Cambridge: Cambridge University Press).
S. SHENOY (1972) 'The Debate, 1931–1971' in F.A. Hayek, *A Tiger by the Tail* (London: Institute of Economic Affairs) pp. 1–12.
R.J. SHILLER (1978) 'Rational Expectations and the Dynamic Structure of Macroeconomic Models: A Critical Review', *Journal of Monetary Economics*, vol. 4, no. 1, 1–44.
R. SKILDELSKY (ed.) (1977) *The End of the Keynesian Era* (London: Macmillan).
A.P. THIRLWALL (1981) 'Keynesian Employment Theory Is Not Defunct', *The Three Banks Review*, no. 131 (September) 14–29.
J. TOMLINSON (1981) *Problems of British Economic Policy 1870–1945* (London: Methuen).
S.C. TSIANG (1947) *The Variations of Real Wages and Profit Margins in Relation to the Trade Cycle* (London: Isaac Pitman).
A.A. WALTERS (1986) *Britain's Economic Renaissance: Margaret Thatcher's Reforms 1979–1984* (New York: Oxford University Press).
P. WILES (1973) 'Cost Inflation and the State of Economic Policy', *Economic Journal*, vol. 83 (June) 377–98.
T. WILSON (1940) 'Capital Theory and the Trade Cycle', *Review of Economic Studies* (June) 169–79.
T. WILSON and P.W.S. ANDREWS (eds) (1951) *Oxford Studies in the Price Mechanism* (Oxford: Clarendon Press).

Index

accelerator principle 58
aggregate demand 90, 91, 97, 98, 117, 120, 126, 127
  deficiency in 115
  management 4, 5, 60, 92, 101–10, 118, 126, 127, 129
Andrews, P.W.S. 118, 148
arbitrage 135
Artis, M.J. 97, 144
asset(s)
  interest-bearing 41, 43, 81, 89
  money 13, 56, 82, 95
  portfolio adjustment of 43, 65–7, 74, 76, 113, 143
  wealth 47, 50, 141
  see also under bank, reserve assets
  see also money, asset demand for
Austrian School, the 2, 30, 123, 127–8, 141, 143

balance of payments
  accounts 98
  as an economic problem 97–9
  automatic adjustment of 87–8, 94
  balance for official financing 9, 90
  fundamental disequilibrium in 90
  monetary theory of the *see under* monetary theory
balance of trade doctrine 85
bank(s)
  borrowing: private sector 71, 75, 77–8, 80; government 72, 75–7, 107, 128
  cash to deposit ratio 14–15
  central 11, 79, 89–90
  cheques 12, 76, 78
  commercial 12, 13, 14, 76–7, 80, 141
  country 11
  credit 13–15, 25, 26, 33, 38, 46, 56, 57, 62–3, 77–80, 88, 89, 103, 141; government control of 78–9, 82, 137; impact upon income distribution 56, 38; impact upon interest rates 32, 46–7; impact upon the money supply 12–15; multiplier 14, 15, 77
  deposits 13, 48, 62, 76, 78, 139
  failures 12
  liquidity requirements of 77
  London clearing 11
  overdrafts 79, 114
  notes *see under* money
  reserve assets 33, 76–7, 78, 80–1
  reserve ratio 14, 80, 81, 135
  special attribute of 63
  see also banking
Bank Charter Act 1844 15
Bank of England 11, 12, 27, 79, 87, 102, 137
Bank Rate 28, 79, 135
banking 17, 92, 114
  deregulation of 81–3
  regulation of 78–81
  reserve 13–15, 88
  see also bank(s)
Banking School, the 78–9
Barry, N.P. 144
barter 8, 12, 19, 111, 114
Bentham, J. 32, 33
Beveridge, Sir William 118
bills of exchange 10, 78
Blaug, M. 85, 144
Bodin, J. 17
Bootle, R. 79
bonds
  price of 43–4, 68, 76–7
  yield on 46, 64
Bretton Woods 89–90, 93, 94, 102
budgetary policy 27, 29, 71–3, 75, 82, 91, 99, 102, 112, 135
  see also credit policy; fiscal policy; monetary policy
business confidence 51, 53
business cycle(s) 33–9, 58

Callaghan, J. 118
Cambridge equation *see under* money
Cambridge School, the 131
Cantillon R. 33, 142
capital 33, 57, 58, 59, 61, 132
  cost of 35
  exports of 87, 92, 95
  human 143
  marginal efficiency of 35–6, 50, 60, 125
  structure of industry 34–6
  shallowing 35–7
  widening 35–7
  see also investment

capitalism 2, 6, 54, 105, 123, 126, 128, 129, 132
Carter, M. 109, 147
cash 12, 13, 135, 137
  see also coins; currency; legal tender; money
Challis, C.E. 9, 144
Charles II 10
Chick, V. 144
Churchill, W.S. 29, 142
Clark, C. 53, 144
Clayton, G. 144
Coddington, A, 110, 144
coins
  fiat value of 9
  see also cash; currency; legal tender; money
collective bargaining *see* wage bargaining
colonial era, the 127
commodities
  prices of 33–5, 37–8, 62
  speculation in 43, 132
  yield from 49-50, 64
concertina effect *see* Hayek on the Ricardo effect
Congdon, T. 10, 144
consumption 25, 26, 32, 34, 41, 43, 53, 56, 58, 63, 107, 129, 132
  goods 57–60
  propensity, 143
  see also commodities
credit
  as distinguished from money 62–3, 77
  non-bank 63
  policy 72, 75, 78, 90
  see also bank credit
crowding out 107–8
Cunliffe Committee, Report of 27
currency 10–12, 111
  convertibilty of 11–12, 27–8, 78–9, 88–9
  debasement of 9, 88
  depreciation of 131–2, 136
  international reserve 83, 89, 90–1
  markets 135–6
  paper 7, 10, 45–6, 78, 88
  reserves, foreign *see* gold and foreign currency reserves
  speculation 136
  see also cash; coins; legal tender; money; sterling
Currency School, the 78–9

Currie, D.A. 97, 144

deflation 27, 28, 29, 62, 89, 126, 132, 136, 141
demand management *see* aggregate demand management
deregulation 16, 78–80, 81
discounted cash flow 36
dollar *see under* USA
Dorn, J.A. 20, 131, 144, 155
Dornbusch, R. 144

economic efficiency 27, 34, 75, 85, 98, 105, 113, 116
  impact of government on 5, 124, 128–30
effective demand *see under* Keynes
efficient market theory, the 95, 105, 106, 125
Eltis, W.A. 143
employment 3, 53, 54, 58, 60, 115, 127, 128, 131
  full, assumption of 23, 26, 27, 28, 46, 105
exchange rate(s) 134
  adjustment 90–1, 95
  fixed rates 87, 93–7, 102
  floating rates 94, 99
  in the post-1945 period 90–2, 93
  overshoot 95–6
  policy 5, 28–9
  purchasing power parity theory of 135
  targeting versus monetary control 94–7, 136-8
expectations 95–7, 126
  formation of 103–4, 125
  inflationary 70–1, 119, 135, 141
  rational 3, 104–9
exports 85–7, 98

Federal Reserve Board 29
Fender, J. 41, 144
financial intermediaries 80
financial markets 75, 81, 96, 124
  linkages with real sectors 48, 95–6
  monetary impact of 71–3, 109, 119, 128
fiscal policy 4, 47, 52, 54, 57, 71, 75, 91, 102, 105, 119, 126, 128
Fisher, I. 19, 20, 21, 22, 24, 137, 144
Flat Earth Society 16
Fletcher, G.A. 59, 114, 144
foreign exchange 10, 94

Index

controls 94, 99
forward cover of 94
markets 87
see also gold and foreign exchange
foreign trade *see* international trade
Friedman, M. 2, 3, 4, 5, 17, 25, 39, 41, 62, 66–70, 73, 75, 81, 127, 131, 137, 143, 144–5
  on expectations 70, 103
  on indexation 5, 119–20
  on the natural rate of unemployment 142
Full Employment in a Free Society 118

Galbraith, J.K. 29, 145
general equilibrium analysis 60–2, 63
General Theory of Employment, Interest and Money, The see under Keynes
Genoa, Conference of 1922 89
Germany 1
  inflation in 113, 133
Gilbert, J.C. 20, 141, 142, 144, 145
gold 8, 9, 10, 17, 45, 46
  and foreign currency reserves 85, 90, 93, 98
  bullion 10, 12, 86–8
  bullion standard 27, 28, 87–8, 90–1
  convertibility 78
  -exchange standard 88–92
  removal from circulation during war 88
goldsmiths 10, 11, 12, 13
Goodhart, C. 80, 145
Goodhart's Law 80
Gould, J. 9, 145
government
  borrowing 75–7, 107, 128
  debt 29, 76–7
  expenditure *see* public expenditure
  failure 130
  role of 130
  stock *see* bonds
  see also budgetary policy; credit policy; fiscal policy; monetary policy
Great Depression, The 29, 89

Hanson, A.H. 142
Hahn, F. 112, 145
Hayek, F.A. von 2, 3, 30, 31–9, 53, 81, 110, 127, 145–6
  advocacy of competition in the supply of money 82–3
  Monetary Theory and the Trade Cycle 33

  on business cycles 34–9
  on capitalistic methods of production 34
  on forced saving 32–4
  on full employment policies 101
  on Keynes's assumption of unemployed resources 105
  on indexation 119–21
  on inflation 75, 119
  on monetary policy 32, 81–3, 142
  on monetary theory 38, 41
  on the gold standard 9, 90
  on the Quantity Theory of money 31–2
  on the Ricardo effect 34–8
Heathfield, D. 146
Henry VIII 9, 85
Hicks, J.R. 48, 60–1, 112, 146, 147
Hume, D. 17, 20, 141
Hutchinson, T.W. 82, 126, 127, 146

imports 85–7, 94, 98
income 46–7, 53, 54, 56, 57, 60, 114, 118, 132
  and the balance of payments 98–9
  as a surrogate for wealth 67
  distribution of 2, 22, 56, 126
incomes policy 118–19
indexation *see under* inflation
industrialisation 123
inflation 5, 102, 111–21, 128, 141
  and business activity 132–3
  and full employment 53–5
  and income distribution 132, 135
  and indexation 5, 119–21, 127, 137
  and public finance 82, 133–4
  and relative prices 33, 111, 116, 128
  and unemployment 102, 106, 109; *see also* Phillips curves
  cost push 5, 111–12, 118–19
  in Germany 113, 133
  in wartime 27, 112
  stages of 112–13, 134, 143
interest, (rate(s) of) 3, 25, 35, 53, 91, 101–2, 107, 108, 117, 124, 141, 143
  and bond prices 43–4, 64, 77
  and trade deficits 87, 91
  determinants of the 26, 41, 43, 47, 54, 56, 58–64, 76; *see also* Liquidity Preference theory; Loanable Funds theory
  effect of monetary disturbance on *see* saving, forced
  effect on saving 25, 143

international differentials in the   95–6
natural rate   25, 32, 33, 34, 51;
  Wicksell and the   25, 26, 31, 52
market rate   26, 32, 33, 34, 44, 46; and
  expectations   44
money rate   49, 50, 58, 61, 132; as a
  guide to monetary policy   74; as the
  highest yield   50, 51, 64
own rates of   48–9, 64
see also investment
interest rate policy   72, 103
internal rate of return   see under
  investment
international monetary system   90
see also Bretton Woods
International Monetary Fund 90
international trade   10
  and exchange rate policy   5, 85–99,
    135–8; see also exchange rate(s)
  and indebtedness   98–9
  deficit   86–7, 91, 94, 102, 135–6
  impact on the money supply   86–8
  mutual gains from   86
  restrictions on   85, 89
  see also balance of payments
investment   4, 24, 25, 32, 53, 54, 56, 57,
  58, 60, 107, 125, 129, 131, 142, 143
  finance of   57
  internal rate of return on   35–7, 49
  marginal efficiency of   35–7
  rate of profit and   37, 64; see also
    interest rate(s)
  see also capital
IS/LM analysis   50

job search   69–70, 103
Johnson, E.S.   3, 146
Johnson, H.G.   3, 4, 6, 27, 28, 41, 56,
  146
Johnson, President L.B.   91

Kahn, R.F.   17, 21, 22, 112, 141, 146
Kaldor, N.   38, 118, 143, 146
Kennedy, President J.F.   91
Keynes, J.M.   2, 3, 31, 39, 85, 123, 126,
  142, 143, 146
  attack on Classical economics   3, 41,
    47, 58–9
  breach with Robertson   4, 56–9
  contribution to Monetarism   41
  'Economic Consequences of Mr.
    Churchill, The'   29
  *General Theory of Employment,
    Interest and Money, The*   3, 4, 5, 6,
    34, 38, 41–52, 53, 54, 55, 57, 62, 64,
    101, 105, 109, 113, 114, 115, 120,
    125, 126, 131, 138, 142, 143
  on currency speculation   136
  on effective demand   47, 53, 115
  on expectations   109
  on fiscal policy   47, 51–2, 54, 57
  on forced saving   55–8
  on income distribution   126
  on indexation 120, 137
  on inflation 55, 111–18, 117, 131–3
  on mercantilism   101–2
  on monetary policy   47, 51, 54, 131–8
  on money as source of investment
    finance   114, 115
  on restoration of the gold
    standard   209, 136
  on the efficient market theory   125
  on the money economy   41, 101, 114,
    123
  on the multiplier   52, 53–4, 57–60, 114
  on the Quantity Theory   47
  on the socialisation of
    investment   125, 130
  on the speculative demand for
    money   43–4
  on the transactions and precautionary
    demands for money   42, 142
  on tripartite motives for holding
    money   41–7
  on uncertainty   41–2, 43, 51
  proposals for an international reserve
    currency   90–1
  static methodology of   4, 34, 35, 38,
    46, 51, 57, 110
  Tract on Monetary Reform, A   131–8
  Treatise on Money, A   131
  see also Liquidity Preference theory
Keynesian economists   see Keynesianism
Keynesian policies   see Keynesianism
Keynesianism   1, 2, 4, 5, 34, 56, 91, 94,
  97, 109, 110, 111, 114, 124, 127, 128,
  130, 133
  evidence of the 1980s   102–3
Klamer, A.   146
Kregel, J.A.   146

labour
  diminishing returns   4, 57, 114
  productivity of   54, 114, 118
  supply   54
  unions   see trade unions
Laidler, D.   141, 147
Lauderdale, J.M.   32

Index

legal tender 9, 11, 13, 83, 88
Lerner, A. 35, 118, 147
Lester, R.A. 147
liquidity 43, 48, 65, 85, 96
  opportunity cost of 41, 43
  preference 44, 46, 52, 53, 60, 83, 124
  trap 44, 50, 51
liquidity preference theory 3, 47, 48–52, 53, 58, 59–64, 142
loanable funds 26, 61, 62, 63, 64
loanable funds theory 4, 44–5, 47, 48–52, 53, 59–64
Locke, J. 45, 62, 141
London, City of 27
  deregulation of the 16
  money market, the 79
Lucas, R. 102, 147

macroeconomic theory 5, 34, 67, 92, 95, 106, 125–7, 129, 130
Maddock, R. 109, 147
Malthus, T. 32
marginal analysis 47, 118
marginal cost 47, 114
market mechanism 80, 83, 105–6
  allocative efficiency of 75, 85, 129–30
market failure 130
market process 3, 17, 85, 111, 119, 124, 127, 128–30
Marshall, A. 20, 21, 22
Matthews, R.C.O. 147
mercantilism 86, 89, 93, 101–2
Menger, C. 127, 141
microeconomic principles 43, 75, 130
Mill, J.S. 18, 141, 142
mints 9, 10
Mises, L. von 33, 127
  on the stages of inflation 112–13, 143
  regression theorem of 8
Modigliani, F. 63, 147
Monsarrat, N. 1, 147
Monetarism 1, 2, 4, 16, 39, 41, 43, 56, 64, 65–74, 75, 79, 83, 94, 96, 102, 123, 127–8, 131, 134, 143
  and exchange rate targeting 97
  the central propositions of 74
Monetarist Rule, the 31, 83, 97, 137
monetary authority 5, 23, 62, 111
monetary base 78–80
monetary instability 94–6
  long-term effects of 28, 41
  short-term effects of 28, 30, 41
monetary economy *see* money economy, the

monetary expansion 4, 90, 91, 113, 134
  effect on bond prices 64, 68
  effect on income distribution 38, 56, 142
  effect on liquidity attribute of money 51
  effect on prices 3, 80, 103, 113, 128
  effect on real sectors 3, 20, 24, 26, 27, 30, 32, 37, 54, 71, 74, 105, 107, 116
  effect on relative prices 3, 31, 32–3, 111, 127, 116
  effect on the rate of interest 25, 37
  effect on the structure of production 4, 33, 34–8
  see also inflation
monetary policy 2, 4, 5, 15–16, 31–2, 62, 71–3, 75, 90, 94–7, 105, 106, 119, 128, 132, 134–8, 141
monetary stability 16, 27, 97
monetary theory 28, 30, 38, 64, 65, 69, 85
  of balance of payments adjustment 85, 93–4
money 7–16, 19, 48–50, 125
  and income 45–7
  and inflation 86, 111–2
  and prices 8, 19, 20, 24, 31, 95, 102, 134; direct transmission mechanism between 24; indirect transmission mechanism between 25–6
  and the rate of interest 25, 44–7
  and the real economy 3, 20, 24, 48
  and uncertainty 125
  as distinguished from credit 62–3
  as a source of investment funds 59, 114
  as a medium of exchange 7, 8, 12, 41, 78
  balances 28, 22, 24, 56, 113
  Cambridge equation, the 19, 20–2, 23, 42, 45, 141
  commodity money 7, 9–11, 12, 86
  demand and supply 15, 21–3, 60, 141
  demand to hold 8, 15, 22–4, 26, 28, 93, 127, 134–5; asset 65–7; precautionary and transactions motives for 41, 42, 142; speculative motive for the 42, 43–4, 65–7, 142; *see also* Keynes, on tripartite motives for holding money
  economy, the 8, 17, 41, 88, 101, 123
  liquidity premium of 51, 52
  high-powered 14, 80–1, 142
  market equilibrium 23, 24, 26, 80

Index

multiplier 14, 81
neutrality of 3, 20, 32, 41, 105
notes and coins 14, 48, 63, 77, 78, 79, 113, 133, 139
  optimal quantity of 83
  price of 63
  purchasing power of 7, 8, 15, 23–4, 50, 112–3, 127–8
  Quantity Theory of 2, 3, 5, 6, 15, 16, 17–30, 31, 38, 41, 44, 46, 54, 55, 56, 58, 61, 86, 94, 127, 131, 134–5; 'naive' 23–4; 'sophisticated' 24–6, 34
  running cash notes 11
  state monopoly of 9, 82
  substitutes 5, 79, 80–2
  supply 14, 21, 45, 46, 50, 81, 107, 113; control of 75–83, 94, 143; definition of 71–3, 76, 139–40, 80, 81, 83; impact of foreign trade on 87–8, 91, 94, 101; impact of government bank-borrowing on 75–7, 107, 128; statistical measures of 81, 83; *see also under* international trade
  token money 3, 7, 10, 11–12, 13, 14, 85, 86–7
  utility of 50
  velocity of circulation of 81, 134; income 21, 65, 67; transactions 18
  Yale equation, the 141
  see also bank credit; cash; coins; currency; legal tender; liquidity
moneyness 16, 48
Moss, L. 7, 31, 35, 147
multiplier, the 52, 53–4, 57–62, 114
Munn, T. 86, 108
Muth, J. 104, 147

National Debt, the 103, 134, 136
national socialism 129
needs-of-trade, the 79, 80
Neftci, S. 106, 147
New Classical School 3, 5, 104, 107, 108, 110
New York Stock Exchange 29, 89, 124
notes and coins *see under* money

O'Driscoll, J.P. 147

Patinkin, D. 8, 142, 147
Phelps, E.S. 69, 70, 103, 147
Phillips, A.W. 147

Phillips curves 68–9, 103, 106, 109, 115
Pigou, A.C. 20, 22, 141
Presley, J.R. 32, 33, 56, 58, 131, 147
price mechanism *see* market mechanism
price(s)
  general level of 3, 19, 31, 50, 68
  index of 127–8, 137
  rigidities 109
  relative 8, 19, 33, 41
producer-interest 129
privatisation 129–30
PSBR *see* public sector borrowing requirement
public expenditure 34, 46, 52, 54, 55, 91, 104, 107–8, 114, 124, 128, 137, 139
public investment 2, 41, 115
public sector borrowing requirement 71–3, 77, 81, 139–40

Quantity theory of money *see under* money

rational expectations *see under* expectations
Rees-Mogg, W. 111, 113, 147
reflux, law of 79
regresion theorem *see under* Mises
Reichsbank 113
Report of the Committee on the Working of the Monetary System 15, 147
Ricardo, D. 32, 142
Ricardo effect *see under* Hayek
Robertson, D. 4, 32, 55–6, 58, 59, 110, 147
Robinson, A. 91, 148
Rothbard, L. 8, 111, 148
Rueff, J. 90, 148

save, propensity to 56, 60, 63
saving(s) 24–5, 26, 31, 34, 43, 107, 131
  forced 3, 4, 31–4, 38, 53–64, 103, 142, 143; induced 55–6
Schumpeter, J. 1, 17, 32, 62, 129, 142, 148
Schwartz, A.J. 144, 145
Sedgwick, R. 144
seigniorage 9, 10
Selective Employment Tax 118
Shackle, G.L.S. 61, 123, 148
Shenoy, S. 119, 148
Shiller, J. 109, 148
silver 8, 10, 17, 86
Sinclair, P.J.N. 144

Index

Skidelskey, R. 148
Smith, A. 82
socialism 129–30
specie flow mechanism 5, 85, 94, 95
sterling 27, 28, 78, 87, 89, 136
  crises 91, 102
  devaluation of 27, 91
Stewart, D. 32
stock market 43
  see also New York Stock Market
Stockton, Lord 127, 144

tâtonnement 61
taxation 75, 107, 111, 130, 133, 134, 139
technocracy 123
Thirlwall, A.P. 114, 148
Thomas, S. 106, 147
Thornton, H. 32, 33, 141, 142
Times, The 143
Tooke, T. 79, 143
thrift 54, 58–60
Tomlinson, J. 27, 148
Torrens, R. 32
Tory Reform Group 143
Tract on Monetary Reform, A see under Keynes
trade cycle *see* business cycles
trade unions 111, 117, 119, 129
Treasury, The 27, 29, 103, 137
Trevithick, J.A. 143, 146
Tsiang, S.C. 148

UK
  currency convertibility in the 1920s 89
  deflation in the 1920s 28, 29, 89
  balance of payments problems 97–9
  stop–go budgetary policy 99
  unemployment 3, 4, 37–8, 47, 51, 56, 108, 114, 115, 126, 143
    and inflation 102, 106, 109, 121, 132; *see also* Phillips curves
    and trade unions 111
    benefits 27, 98
    equilibrium 52, 101, 110
    frictional 70
    in the 1920s 27–9
    in the 1930s 36, 54, 103, 105
    involuntary 54, 57, 115
    natural rate of 25, 31, 141, 142
USA
  bank failures in 29
  budgets in late 1960s 90
  dollar: as a reserve currency 89, 90–1; suspension of convertibility 91
  post-war trade deficits 91

Vaughn, K. 31, 35
velocity of circulation *see under* money

wage(s)
  bargaining 103, 109, 111, 118; and inflation 119–21; *see also* trade unions
  goods 4, 54, 120
  money 33, 54, 126; stickiness of 50, 52
  real 121; and unemployment 54, 114; reductions in 4, 57, 103, 114, 126
  relativities 111, 112, 115–16, 119, 121
  reservation 70
  rigidities 121, 116
  see also Phillips curves
Wall Street *see* New York Stock Exchange
Walrasian system 61
Walters, A.A. 97
war 112, 113, 124, 123, 131
  First World 12
  Napoleonic 11
  Second World 5, 10, 89, 103
Wealth of Nations, The 82
Weber, W. 146
Wicksell, K. 25, 26, 31, 32, 33, 141, 142
  see also under interest rate
Wiles, P. 112, 148
Wilson, T. 38, 118, 148

Yale equation, the *see under* money